Sugar and Spice
and No Longer
Nice

Deborah Prothrow-Stith
Howard R. Spivak

Foreword by Janet Reno

Sugar and Spice and No Longer Nice

How We Can Stop Girls' Violence

JOSSEY-BASS
A Wiley Imprint
www.josseybass.com

Published by Jossey-Bass
A Wiley Imprint
989 Market Street, San Francisco, CA 94103-1741   www.josseybass.com

Jossey-Bass books and products are available through most bookstores. To contact Jossey-Bass
directly call our Customer Care Department within the U.S. at 800-956-7739, outside the
U.S. at 317-572-3986, or fax 317-572-4002.

Jossey-Bass also publishes its books in a variety of electronic formats. Some content that appears
in print may not be available in electronic books.

Library of Congress Cataloging-in-Publication Data
Prothrow-Stith, Deborah, date.
  Sugar and spice and no longer nice : how we can stop girls' violence / Deborah Prothrow-Stith,
Howard R. Spivak ; foreword by Janet Reno.
    p. cm.
  Includes bibliographical references and index.
  ISBN-13 978-0-7879-7571-5 (alk. paper)
  ISBN-10 0-7879-7571-0 (alk. paper)
  1. Girls—Psychology. 2. Girls—Social conditions. 3. Violence in children. 4. Violence in
adolescence. I. Spivak, Howard R., date. II. Title.
  HQ777.P76 2005
  303.6'0835'20973—dc22   2005003708

Printed in the United States of America
FIRST EDITION
HB Printing   10 9 8 7 6 5 4 3 2 1

Contents

Foreword

During my service as attorney general of the United States, I became familiar with the work of the authors of this book, both of whom are recognized as leaders in violence prevention. Deborah Prothrow-Stith is known as a pioneer in the effort to address violence as a public health problem, and Howard R. Spivak is nationally known for his violence prevention work in the American Academy of Pediatrics and the medical community. Their studies have reinforced my belief that much of youth violence can be prevented if we make an investment in our children of love, time, understanding, support, and direction. We cannot solve the problem of youth violence simply by punishing the perpetrators. We must focus on preventing the occurrence of violence in the first place, and we must provide programs in the juvenile justice system to prepare perpetrators to return to the community with improved chances of success.

The authors' first book, *Murder Is No Accident,* is a primer for understanding factors that either put children at risk for or protect them from violence. They describe experiences and strategies that can help individuals, families, and communities establish a practical youth violence prevention effort. Their work in the city of Boston serves as a model for other communities across the nation. In this book the authors highlight the increase in arrests of girls for violence and the concern expressed by educators and others over this disturbing trend.

In *Sugar and Spice and No Longer Nice,* the authors deal primarily with girls' violence and warn that we must focus on the prevention of violence and creation of reentry programs for girls at risk of committing violence. The book stresses that if we act quickly, we have a chance to contain violent behavior before it gets out of hand, as it did with boys.

This very personal book reflects the authors' own struggle with the issue. They present practical approaches that grow from their professional and personal trials and their experiences as doctors, public health practitioners, and citizens. They understand the complexities of raising girls into young women. They appreciate the stresses, joys, and dilemmas facing parents, teachers, and extended family who are raising girls in today's society. Having made their own mistakes, learned lessons the hard way, and struggled through the process of raising their own daughters, they have come through it all with a rich understanding of the problems girls face in our society today. Girls' violence has grown to include girls from all communities and economic settings and encompasses physical fighting, dangerous hazing, and gang-related activities.

The authors point to the trend in entertainment media that is redefining femininity and values through increasingly violent female heroes as one cause of growing violence among girls. They also suggest that our communities and the criminal justice system have failed to develop adequate programs to address the needs of girls. Parents, teachers, and extended family must provide role models for girls that give them options to follow and skills that enable them to live by nonviolent values. We must work with our criminal justice system to develop programs that promote understanding and guidance, not just punishment.

This book provides solid insights and strategies for addressing girls' violence before it gets out of hand. Listed in the Resources at the end of the book are an array of services and organizations that can help. I applaud these authors' work, commitment, and their heartfelt and practical advice.

Janet Reno
Attorney General of the United States,
1993–2001

*For all the girls of America, present and future, who deserve
no less than a world without violence, and*

*With love to Mildred, my role model; Lady Percy, who taught me
how to dance and to roll my hair; and Mimi, my delight*
—DP-S

*With love to the three women who have truly enriched my life:
Ida, Janet, and Zoë*
HRS

Acknowledgments

We have many people to thank for their contributions to our work over the years. Several have inspired the content of this book and assisted with its completion.

First and foremost, we want to acknowledge and thank the many, many people dedicated to violence prevention across the nation. Every day these individuals seek every opportunity possible to prevent violence. They are the parents, politicians, teachers, clergy, public health workers, neighbors, and teens for whom we have written this book. As we have done constantly since the beginning of our work with survivors of violence, we must thank them again and again. Their energy and commitment are constant sources of inspiration to us. They are the heart and the soul of the violence prevention movement. We look to them for direction and guidance and hope that we have given them half as much as they have given us.

A well-deserved thank-you to our families is also essential, as they have been a crucial part of any success that we have had. For two decades they have been believers in our work and supporters of the cause. We offer particular thanks to Mimi Stith for reading the manuscript of this book and sharing her thoughts and comments. We also acknowledge Zoë Spivak and Mimi for their insights and challenges over their growing-up years. Several friends deserve acknowledgment as well—we thank Rita Nethersole and Meagan Julian for reviewing and commenting on this book and pushing us for clarity and focus.

Our assistants, Micki Diegel and Venetta Armstrong (also a friend and graduate student), contributed in concrete ways to the publication of this book. Venetta deserves particular mention for her extensive reading and editing efforts.

Alan Rinzler, our editor, believed in this project when things were still fuzzy to us and wrote us a couple of "Dear People" e-mails to keep us on track. We thank him for his tenacity and capacity to stick with us.

Finally, we are grateful to the parents who struggle each day to raise their children so they become healthy, happy, nonviolent adults. We wrote this book in the hope that they would find it helpful in their labor of love.

Deborah Prothrow-Stith
Howard R. Spivak
Boston, Massachusetts

Sugar and Spice and No Longer Nice

Part One

Understanding
the Challenge

Chapter One

We Have a Problem

LITTLE GIRLS
What are little girls made of, made of?
What are little girls made of?
Sugar and spice
And everything nice.
That's what little girls are made of.

LITTLE BOYS
What are little boys made of, made of?
What are little boys made of?
Snakes and snails and puppy dog tails.
That's what little boys are made of.

—*Mother Goose nursery rhyme*

Not that it should or ever did, but this nursery rhyme certainly does not describe today's boys and girls. Girls continue to break down barriers and diminish the differences between their level of achievement and that of boys in many areas, and violent behavior is no exception. As society has changed over the years, the differences between the ways little girls and little boys display anger and aggression have shifted as well. Today American girls are showing their mean streaks directly and violently.

In addition to displaying the "hidden" and "indirect" aggression (backbiting, ostracizing others, and hurtful self-directed behaviors) that has been the subject of recent best-selling books and popular talk shows, girls are turning to physical violence as well. Girls have become a part of the epidemic of youth violence—and not just as victims. Girls are fighting, and they are not just fighting back in self-defense. Girls are fighting like boys—not as much (yet) but with a similar willingness to use physical violence.

Things have changed. There have always been isolated, extraordinary cases of female violence, like the actions of Lizzie Borden[1] or the young women involved with Charles Manson.[2] But the current changes in girls' behavior are not isolated, and they challenge traditional ways of thinking at a very basic level. Parents, extended family, teachers, judges, politicians, neighbors—all of us find it difficult to accept or understand what is happening. It is just too unsettling to acknowledge that girls are committing some of the same horrible acts of violence that boys commit.

Our Motivation

For over a decade now we have been receiving comments and questions about girls' fighting, and they all reflect the same concerns. Middle school principals tell us, "I'm not having as much of a problem with boys fighting as I am having now with girls fighting," or, "The worst fights in my school are among girls," or, "The first time I ever had to call an ambulance to the school was when two girls got into a big fight." Then they ask us why this is happening and what they should do.

The problem is not just a middle school problem either. We get many calls for help from high school teachers and administrators, and we even get occasional calls from colleges and universities. In January 2003, after giving a Martin Luther King Jr. celebration lecture at a state university in the middle of the country, Deborah was asked by the dean of students to participate in a special meeting about six freshman girls who were involved in an ongoing quarrel. The arguments among them had started in September, at the beginning of the school year, and by that January the girls had been involved in three major confrontations (two involved physical contact and one turned into an actual physical fight that had to be broken up). College women! Fighting! Hitting and kicking each other. It didn't seem possible. Needless to say, everyone on campus was talking about the fights, the school administration was perplexed, and no one really knew what to do.

Although such physical fights are still uncommon, this isn't the only request for assistance we have received from colleges and college students' parents. Just the other day Deborah got a call from a friend whose goddaughter was being expelled from college for fighting. For many reasons, we shouldn't have been surprised. Hazing in college athletics, fraternities, and sororities is common and overlooked as a right of passage. Hazing at its best is aggressive behavior and at its worst is a euphemism for violence and brutality. Alcohol is a large problem on college campuses. Drinking can make it more likely that people will act on their aggression and anger. And at all ages, girls and young women are behaving more aggressively and more violently.

Girls Are Different!

Parents, schools, and communities must take girls' differences into account to be effective in their roles. Responses to girls' violence must reflect these differences as well. Parents, communities, and any others who serve girls cannot develop violence prevention efforts based solely on their experiences with boys. The criminal justice system cannot successfully treat girls who commit violence using exactly what is used for boys, although that is the common practice at this time. From experience we know that will not work. The consequences and costs to society will be severe if all of us continue to do this.

Girls Are Not That Different!

In addition to their obvious biological differences, girls and boys are traditionally socialized very differently. Yet many of these socialization differences are lessening, as illustrated by girls' participation in sports, enhanced academic opportunities, and expanded job possibilities. When it comes to the portrayal of violent behavior in the entertainment media, the differences have disappeared completely. Movies and children's TV programming, including cartoons, regularly portray the female superhero as violent and sexy. We call this "the feminization of the superhero" (or *supershero*). As the entertainment media equalized the violent behavior of male and female superheroes, we expected the behaviors of real girls and boys to equalize as well over time. And they have.

We chose to write this book to provide information in a manner that is accessible to everyone. We hope this information will help parents, teachers, and other adults who love and serve children. We want to better inform those who work with girls so that they understand girls' differences and respond more appropriately to their needs. We want parents, educators, community leaders, those addressing public policy issues, and others who serve girls to become better prepared for and effective at preventing girls from engaging in violence and responding to girls who are already involved in violence.

Through real-life stories and scientific data, we suggest strategies to make things better for girls at home, in school, and in other settings. All the stories we present are based on real events and reflect the experiences of real people. In some cases these stories are composites of several situations in order to illustrate a range of issues. Of course we do not use real names or settings; we wish to respect the privacy of those who have shared their stories with us over the last two decades. We are most grateful to all of them (colleagues, teachers, friends, and especially our patients and the teens we have served) for sharing with us so that we can share with you.

A Teacher's Story

We first met Ellen at a New England conference on youth violence in 1997, the year of her retirement. During the discussion after our presentation, she asked the then-familiar question, "What is going on with girls, and what can we do about it?" However, before either of us could respond, she offered her own ten-minute answer that reflected her personal thoughts, reflections, and experiences. Her insight and passion so impressed us that we sought her out after the session to learn more about her experiences.

At the time, Ellen was a middle school teacher with almost thirty years of experience in a middle-class, predominantly white Boston-area suburb. In addition she had raised two daughters in that community, thus experiencing the changes in the social environment and in the behavior patterns of girls from two vantage points—as a teacher and as a mother. Her comments at the conference summarized three decades of change and brought insights and perspectives that have helped shape our thoughts on the evolving dynamics of girls, aggression, anger, and behavior.

When Ellen first started teaching in the late 1960s, girls were using teasing and name-calling as their primary methods of playing out anger and conflict. Usually, competition over schoolwork, for the attention of others, or during recreational activities such as games and sports remained overtly friendly, with little name-calling that Ellen witnessed. Occasionally she would overhear a girl bragging about some new possession her family had acquired or some accomplishment. She would also see some girls involved in classroom competition for the right answer to a problem. Believe it or not, there was even a little one-upmanship in an effort to be teacher's pet (remember those days?). But as a rule everything went along well, and everybody (with the exception of a few boys) appeared to behave well and get along. Ellen isn't pining for the good old days, however, because she saw some withdrawn and isolated girls as well—girls who were just too quiet and a few girls who seemed to do everything other girls told them to do. Ellen often thought that these girls were troubled or maybe even abused.

During these early days, Ellen could almost always tell when some girls were having a fight or argument by their comments about each other's appearance, clothing, or hairstyle. In some ways it was a verbal form of bullying, but it was not so obvious at the time because the remarks were made with humor and a sweet manner. Ellen now knows that they just appeared to be sweet; the meanness was covered up by an innocent, girlish style that rarely provoked notice or reaction from adults. And maybe these exchanges really weren't so mean after all. They certainly didn't seem to cause the pain of what Ellen saw in later years.

During her first year of teaching, Ellen recalls witnessing a year-long scenario involving two girls who were best friends but who also competed regularly for attention and social status in the class. She could always tell when things were rocky between the two of them by the level of teasing they displayed toward each other. She noted that this teasing behavior was generally most evident when they had an audience of other girls around them,[3] as if they needed others to witness the putdowns and insults. But never did these exchanges reach the point of yelling or even raised voices. Overt anger was not expressed. Any meanness was always indirect and sugarcoated.

Overt Expressions of Aggression Emerge

Although Ellen does not recall seeing other forms of expressed anger, she does remember hearing a number of stories from other teachers about girls who exhibited various forms of self-destructive behaviors that reflect internalized anger. In her fifth year of teaching, she heard for the first time about an eating disorder, from a teacher in the other middle school in her town. From teachers in schools in Boston she began to hear about middle school girls who were running away, acting out sexually, and experimenting with alcohol, but she did not see or hear about such occurrences in her town at that time. However, she was beginning to formulate a picture of a range of behaviors that girls were using to express anger, conflict, depression, and frustration.

Among girls in her community it appeared that these behaviors involved the socially acceptable aggression of teasing and name-calling. She suspected that the more destructive form of this aggression was self-directed and reflected in eating behaviors, withdrawal, and being a pushover. Ellen was aware that these behaviors might also be a sign of a broader range of issues or disorders. And she began to wonder about the acting-out behaviors (cursing, frank name-calling, and alcohol use) that Boston teachers were experiencing—an urban version of what Ellen was seeing among girls in her school. At this early point, Ellen was also seeing signs among boys of increased fighting and outright physical aggression in her suburban school. She also began reading about the more serious violence among teenage and young adult boys in the inner cities across the country. Although she did not realize it at the time, she was beginning to formulate her own version of the progression of violence that was yet to play out over the next three decades. Never did she expect the violence to reach her community, and never did she expect to see girls become as overtly vicious toward each other as they later did.

The next phase that Ellen noticed began about ten years later, in the early 1980s. Though it may have started earlier, she became increasingly aware of a new dynamic involving forced exclusion and social isolation. It looked like a group dynamic, with particular girls singled out and excluded from group activities and social events. She had seen this behavior before, but it was now happening in a more pervasive and regular pattern, and although group related, it almost always had a clear leader and almost always seemed to stem from conflicts between two girls who had a history of friendship. The rejection and exclusion were becoming more visible, and the girls who were the leaders were skillful at persuading other children to single out and turn on another girl. One of Ellen's noteworthy observations was that the girl targeted for exclusion frequently shifted and in many cases would go back and forth between two, sometimes three, girls. These shifts would often be linked to an argument or competitive event. As Ellen had seen with teasing, most of the girls in the class would play the role of observer or follower, with a clear and smaller set of girls, generally those with stronger, more assertive personalities, in the leadership role. The "queen bees" were emerging.

Ellen frequently tells the story of two girls in one of her classes who were the trendsetters in their grade for fashion and social organizing. They had been friends since grade school and were surrounded by a large circle of girls who did almost everything together. During the course of the year, Ellen noted that at any given time, one of the two girls would essentially be in charge of much of the social planning for the group and the other would then frequently be left out of the planning and even the activity. Although the girls acted like friends, their battle for control was played out in a rather mean-spirited manner that was often hurtful. Ellen noted that often one or the other girl (depending on who was up and who was down) would appear in her classroom after school crying or just needing to talk. She successfully negotiated reconciliations throughout the year only to witness the reappearance of the negative behaviors with each new conflict. She also became aware that both of these girls came from families with considerable conflict. She began to wonder about the role that family conflict and problems might be playing in the girls' attraction to each other as friends and their ways of dealing with their conflicts with each other. Observing and assisting these girls, Ellen was beginning to think about underlying factors that might contribute to their learning behaviors that were increasingly more aggressive.

Ellen made the point to us that in the early 1980s this kind of behavior was still relatively isolated to a couple of girls. It was still pretty subtle and well within the boundaries of socially acceptable behavior for girls. She was not yet seeing evidence of the physical aggression that was increasingly apparent among the boys in her school. Girls were still acting like girls; boys were the bigger problem and were getting the adults' attention with respect to disciplinary consequences and concerns.

Girls' Repertoire Expands: Bullying, Putdowns, and Power Plays

By the early 1990s the next trend appeared, in the form of a jump in aggressive behavior and meanness—bullying. Bullying was a phenomenon Ellen had witnessed and been concerned about with respect to boys for quite a while. But she had seen little if any such behavior among girls. Then during the late 1980s, she began to see a dramatic presence of bullying and more aggressive victimization among girls. A kind of *meanness* had emerged, seemingly from nowhere. Rather than being content to be the queen bee for a moment and to have that designation move from one girl to the next depending on the activity and whose turn it was to be in charge, a few girls, Ellen noted, were consolidating power, doing everything possible to hold on to that power and becoming more and more vicious with their putdowns. It was no longer enough for girls to put down their competitors; now they were figuratively stomping on them while they were down and making sure they were unable to get up. The atmosphere in the school was truly beginning to feel like girl-eat-girl.

What was also different was that this behavior occurred less often among girls who were friends and more often among girls with different levels of power, based on physical attributes, personality, social status, or occasionally academic skills. Compared to earlier displays of competitiveness, this seemed to be more a display of strength versus weakness.

As they were among boys, these behaviors seemed to be recurrent and to involve clearly recognizable groups: those who bullied, those who were bullied, and—the largest group—those who just stood by. The bullies were often the most popular girls, those who experienced considerable social success, even though they were not necessarily liked by many of their peers. Those bullied were often the least socially accepted (sometimes by race and class measures) and were generally on the shy end of the personality spectrum.

Bullied children were usually different from the majority in some way and often had the most difficulty fitting in.

Ellen noted two other elements that deeply concerned her. The first was the growing presence of violent and aggressive role models in the popular media, especially movies and TV. The second was her increasing awareness of certain family and social dynamics surrounding the girls involved in the bullying behaviors (both those who bullied and those who were bullied).

Ellen Reaches Out for Help

Although she did not quite know yet what to make of the media and role model influences, Ellen was clear that there were factors in girls' family and social environments that were, at the very least, contributing to their roles as either bullies or victims. In her role as a confidant for many girls, Ellen became increasingly aware of difficult family situations, disruptive family conflict, harsh disciplinary practices, and general family dysfunction. She began to wonder about the relationships between these family settings and the behaviors she was seeing at school.

Ellen began to seek out research related to the behaviors she was witnessing, but she became frustrated at how little she could find that focused on girls. Although much was written about boys and their risk factors for aggression, fighting, and bullying, there was almost nothing about girls. Although there were articles about boys and violent media, again, there was almost nothing about girls. Ellen felt pretty much on her own in trying to understand what she was seeing. Her efforts to seek advice and insight from peers in education as well as friends in the mental health profession were met with shrugs. Others had similar stories, but no one seemed to know what, if anything, to do. In mental health, for example, the primary focus was on girls' self-destructive behaviors in the form of eating disorders, suicide attempts, substance use, and self-abusive behaviors. With respect to violence, the primary focus was on the victimization of girls in the context of dating and domestic violence. Ellen knew these were important issues but was still concerned about the almost total lack of attention to the issue of aggression and violence among girls. She feared that violence among girls was developing a pattern that would mirror the decade-long progression of violence seen among boys across the nation.

Ellen's shared her experiences with us at a time when we were beginning to receive questions about girls' behavior from teachers and school administrators at our presentations all over the country. Our concerns about a new wave in the youth violence epidemic were growing. Yet, like Ellen, we found little research to advance our thinking about the events teachers and administrators were witnessing, and many of our colleagues dismissed our concerns as an overreaction to anecdotes—stories from individuals that might reflect only isolated incidents and a small problem.

The Rise of Physical Violence

The last and most recent chapter of Ellen's story concerns her experience in the mid-1990s, when she saw verbal and nonviolent behaviors start to shift into physical aggression and fighting. It was also in the mid-1990s that the headmaster of a high school in the Midwest said to us that he had never had to call an ambulance in response to a fight at school until girls started fighting. Not surprisingly, we were more than a bit taken aback by this comment until we heard similar comments several more times from other principals in other places. It was at this time that Ellen was beginning to see and have to break up near fights between girls in her classroom. She remembers the first actual fight. During her last year of teaching, two girls started fighting over the rumor that one had spread about the other, calling her a "slut." For urban boys (and more recently girls), insulting someone's mother is asking for a fight. For suburban girls, it's calling her a slut.

Understanding the Changes

We know that anecdotes don't tell you much about the big picture; they tell you the details of one event or one set of experiences. You have to look at data like school suspensions, juvenile arrests, or surveys of girls to get the big picture. Yet we have learned that the real-life stories are hugely important because they let you know what is happening long before the numbers do. Also, stories help you interpret the big picture, especially when the stories come from young people, parents, and school-based professionals—the front line.

We learned this from dealing with the second wave of youth violence. The first wave occurred in the early 1980s, mostly among young men in poor communities in cities of more than five hundred thousand. The second wave was the one that hit America's middle class in suburban and rural towns in the late 1980s and early 1990s. At the time when we were growing increasingly concerned that this second wave of youth violence was in the making, we were faced with denial and numbers that lagged behind the stories about violence. Yet we were getting more and more invitations to speak in smaller towns and suburban communities, and we kept hearing the stories there. When the suburban school shootings began in the early 1990s, we knew what was happening. Many of our colleagues thought these shootings were isolated events and denied the possibility of a second wave; they didn't have the benefit of the stories. (And the second wave continues to affect smaller towns. Preliminary numbers from the FBI for 2003 indicate that cities of less than 50,000 had greater increases in homicides—4 to 15 percent—than did larger cities (all with less than 1 percent increase).[4] When you put current stories together with the data and the patterns from the past, it is easier to interpret the trends ahead.

Ellen's experiences as a teacher over thirty years have helped us to interpret the numbers and tie together several important lessons we have learned. Ellen witnessed girls' aggressive behaviors progress from name-calling toward more and more violent behavior. This country experienced a similar progression among boys as well; fifty years ago teachers' biggest behavioral concerns were chewing gum, talking out of turn, and joking around. Now talking back, swearing, and fighting are major concerns, and teachers are worried about getting physically hurt while trying to stop a student fight or having students direct violence at them. Most of this bad behavior is still displayed by boys. However, the same progression toward more vicious and more violent behavior is being seen among girls.

As a society, we can ignore Ellen's experience. We can pretend that it is only certain girls in certain neighborhoods—an isolated problem. We can pretend that it will stay contained to the really "deviant" and somehow "abnormal" girls. Or we can learn from our experiences with boys, understand the patterns now occurring with girls, and commit ourselves to responding with real and comprehensive prevention efforts.

The Fate of the Bird:
Developing a Prevention Focus

Stories are just that, stories. There have always been tales of horrific crimes committed by girls, and there is no shortage of unusual classroom stories. The fundamental question is what if anything is different? Do the principals' comments and teachers' stories that we have heard across the country add up to anything more than stories? Do the numbers show any measurable changes in girls' behavior? The answers are yes, yes, and yes. Something has changed. Girls and young women are fighting more, and in Chapter Three we share some of the numbers with you.

What do the changes in girls' behavior mean? How are girls and boys different? These are questions we address in Chapters Four and Five. What are parents to do? What can school and educators do? What can communities do? How do we reverse the trends? These questions are addressed in the last four chapters of the book.

Are the changes in girls' behavior permanent? That we don't know. However, the story of a boy who wanted to outsmart the Wise Old Soul of his village comes to mind.[5] The boy's scheme was to ask the Wise Old Soul this question: "Is the bird I am holding in my hand dead or alive?" If the Wise Old Soul answered "dead," the boy would open his hand and let the bird fly away. If the Wise Old Soul answered "alive," the boy would close his hand tightly and crush the bird. Either way, the boy would prove that he was smarter than the Wise Old Soul. As planned, the boy confronted the village elder and asked, "Is the bird I am holding in my hand dead or alive?" Much to the boy's disappointment, the Wise Old Soul's response was, "The fate of that bird is in your hands."

Are the changes permanent? We don't know. But we do believe in individual and collective action. We have seen the positive impact of deliberate and sustained community action in reducing youth homicide rates in Boston. We wrote about this community effort in our first book together, *Murder Is No Accident*. The current change in girls' behavior is significant enough for us to issue a warning and offer strategies. That is why we wrote this book. We think like the old soul in the tale; the fate of this bird is in the hands of all of us.

It is clear to most people who work directly with children and adolescents that girls' behavior has changed and that girls' violence is now a significant concern in America; yet our society continues to act on an outdated paradigm: boys are violent and girls are made of "sugar and spice and everything nice." Our schools, courts, and youth prevention programs have not responded appropriately with gender-specific violence prevention activities. They are finding it difficult to understand what the changes mean and even more difficult to know what to do about them. Parents and teachers are struggling to understand what is going on and what they can do.

Before this new wave of girls' participating in the epidemic of youth violence increases even more, all of us must acknowledge and confront the issue. As a society, we must take the necessary steps to help our girls as well as our boys. Most important, parents are central to addressing this growing problem and they should have information, guidance, and options. Parents must help their daughters grow up safely and healthy—nonvictim and nonviolent.

Life's Most Difficult Job

We ourselves are parents, and in this book we share some of our personal stories as well. We each have a daughter (Deborah's daughter, Mimi, is twenty-three and Howard's daughter, Zoë, is twenty-two) and a son (Deborah's son is Percy and Howard's son is Lee). We are not holding our children up as examples nor are we saying that we are model parents. But we are combining our professional and personal experiences to better share some knowledge and ideas with you.

Adolescence is a difficult time, and it is getting more and more difficult for girls. Constant media portrayals of sexy and, increasingly, violent images coupled with new levels of freedom and access to information and the influences of others via the Internet—add up to a bigger challenge for parents. It sometimes feels overwhelming for all of us raising teenage daughters.

Parents are often perplexed by what and what not to do in raising their children. It used to be that you didn't have to worry too much about girls. Once the biggest worry for parents of girls was pregnancy. When we say things have changed, it's an understatement. So how does the art of parenting change to keep up? What should you do and what shouldn't you do as the parent of a girl? How do you make sure she is assertive *and* not aggressive? How do you make sure that she is nonviolent *but also* nonvictim? What are the tips that can help?

The ART of Parenting

In Chapter Six, we describe the ART model of parenting for raising girls. It pulls together in a simple format the work of many people who have studied and written about parenting and girls. It is by no means all-inclusive, but it does serve as a good framework for getting the help you need as a caring parent and providing your children with the help they need.

ART is an acronym:

A: Act as a role model—do rather than tell; demonstrate rather than dictate.

R: Reach out to others—build a community of caring adults around your child.

T: Talk and listen—communicate, communicate, and communicate some more.

No matter the age of your daughter, you can put the ART model into practice. In Chapter Six, we will discuss acting as a role model for your child; reaching out to others who can assist you in setting the stage for the teen years; talking and listening and never breaking the lines of communication, no matter how difficult or hurtful it gets for you; and using the in-the-car strategy.

Many parents of today's teens and young adults remember being raised in a fairly tightly knit neighborhood where other adults were expected to take some responsibility for all the neighborhood children—and did so. Now parents have to create that neighborhood or extended family around their children.

There was a time when it was easier to control the information and images a child saw. Now it's harder to do so. As society allows commercial interests in children to be fully exploited, the burden on parents becomes even greater. At the same time that parents have to counter and mitigate the commercial junk and unhealthy images that are advertised to children, they find themselves targeted by political rhetoric blaming them for their children's actions. The role of protecting children is now almost exclusively on the shoulders of parents, and parents need help; the job has gotten harder, and the training for most remains virtually absent.

We see a trend that indicates that parents of girls must now also worry about violence, criminal behavior, and arrests. And we wrote this book because we believe parenting matters. We believe there are effective responses to the things that influence children and their behaviors, responses that are prevention oriented and not limited to threats, spanking, sending a child to her room, and grounding. We believe creativity and action on the part of parents can make a huge difference. We want you to feel empowered by the strategies we put forth—empowered to make a difference, not just in the lives of your children but in your community and nation.

We feel that parents are being blamed for things over which they have no control. We want that to change. We want a society that is much more supportive of your efforts to raise your daughter. Instead of regularly placing tantalizing, unhealthy images in her path or scheduling a school coffee hour with parents in the middle of a workday, a society committed to helping parents would make different decisions. Images of violence and sexual promiscuity would not be shown on after-school and prime-time television. Enough after-school activities would be available so that children would not have to be home alone watching television until a working parent arrives. Because certain changes at the public policy level would also be helpful, in Chapter Eight we present strategies for getting more involved in increasing the level of support for families. While we hope for change in the bigger picture—in media, public policy, and resources for youth programs—we believe this book will help you with the things you do control.

A Call to Action

We must all rise to the challenge, change our attitudes, improve our parenting skills, confront cultural norms and media images, take responsibility for and be concerned about all children, and make sure the schools are doing their part. We can't sit by and leave our children at risk. American society is learning a hard lesson the hard way—no child is immune to violent influences. Despite wishful thinking to the contrary, even girls can be manipulated to behave violently by a toxic environment.

This toxic environment is in part a product of certain adult attitudes and practices:

1. The glorification and "selling" of violence to children by the media and the social culture. We are sometimes asked if it is a good thing that girls are finally standing up for themselves and fighting back. Unfortunately, in a society where standing up for yourself equals violence, that is a reasonable question. Our goal for girls (and boys too) is that they be nonvictim and nonviolent.

2. The false reassurance offered to middle-class suburban families by the unfair stereotype that minority and inner-city girls are the only violent girls. In the past, false reassurances about boys' violence and drug use meant that schools and communities were unprepared to act promptly and failed to prevent epidemics of violence and drug abuse.

3. The significant attention given to stranger violence, which often overshadows efforts to address family, friend, and acquaintance violence. Girls and women are most likely to be victims and perpetrators in settings where they know the others involved. Unfortunately, family, friend, and acquaintance violence receives little news coverage, public policy attention, or private or public resources, even though nearly half of the rapes and the homicides in America involve individuals known to each other.

4. The current boy-oriented approach to violence prevention programs, which ignores the aspects of socialization, vulnerabilities, peer relationships, and family position and the other characteristics that make girls quite different from boys.

5. The boy-oriented practices of the criminal justice system and other community institutions, including schools, which are inadequate to meet the unique challenges facing girls.

These attitudes and practices must change.

This book is a call to action. We in this society are facing a crisis. Before a girl—someone's daughter—commits a national-attention-grabbing, horrible act of violence like the shootings at

Columbine High School, something needs to be done. All of us need to help. Everyone must be involved. The problem is not just for parents or teachers or people living in certain communities to handle. This problem affects us all, and a comprehensive response to save our children is long overdue. From improved parenting skills to better schools to healthier entertainment for our children, the fate of this bird is in our hands.

Chapter Two

Hidden Aggression
Becomes Outward Violence

America experienced a rise in youth violence in the early 1980s that created fear and concern throughout the country. The increase started in poor urban America, among the most vulnerable children, and broadened from there. Now, all over the country, parents, godparents, teachers, politicians, and teens themselves worry about youth violence. We know this because they tell us. We hear expressions of fear, grief, and angst from Los Angeles to Baton Rouge, from Salt Lake City to Portland, Maine, from Akron, Ohio, to our home base in Boston. For twenty years, we have traveled throughout the United States to address youth violence as a public health problem. Fifteen years ago we heard an occasional mention of girls fighting. Ten years ago the stories and concerns changed, and we started getting an earful about girls fighting, particularly from middle school principals and teachers. Person after person began telling us that girls' fights were becoming an alarming problem.

We were told that girls were generally being more aggressive, girls were fighting other girls, and girls were sometimes even fighting boys. News accounts of girls in gangs started appearing with increasing frequency. We were caught off guard. What was happening? Was this change real? Then we turned to the facts and figures and realized that something really had changed. Not only were the stories changing but the numbers were changing too!

In the light of our experience over the last two decades, first with urban boys living in poverty and then with suburban and rural boys, the pattern developing with girls looks like the beginning of another frightening wave of the youth violence epidemic in America. Tragically, the problem has finally reached the most socially resilient group of children—girls. There is not yet a violence epidemic among middle-class white girls, but we see it coming. Now is the time to act. (Actually the time was many years ago, when the youth violence epidemic began and traumatized poor urban communities and families, but that is another book.)

A dramatic increase in youth homicides in the early 1980s marked the beginning of America's youth violence epidemic. The first and largest wave of this epidemic affected boys and young men in poor urban communities, including many black and Hispanic male adolescents. The second wave involved boys and young men in middle-class suburban and rural communities, as exemplified by the suburban school shootings that received national attention. In the late 1990s, violent deaths among youths began to plateau and then declined, primarily because of a decline in urban violence. Now, as the second wave also seems to be declining, there are clear signs of a third wave of the epidemic—among girls and young women.[1] And perhaps there is a fourth wave on the horizon, involving younger and younger children.

The Third Wave:
Moving from Denial to Understanding

Parents and adults with daily responsibilities for girls must recognize this third wave and engage in new strategies for preventing violence among girls. Unfortunately, considerable denial and an unwillingness to acknowledge the changes in girls' behavior exist. People seem to minimize, make excuses for, or explain away girls' violence, perhaps because it is too difficult to accept. For a variety of reasons, girls' fighting goes against the expectations and sensibilities of most people.

Although it is clear that girls are fighting in unprecedented numbers and ways, the problem hasn't quite reached suburban middle-class communities—yet. And, as we saw with boys' violence, national concern about problems doesn't seem to emerge until middle America feels vulnerable. This creates unfortunate delays in prevention efforts.

No essays on fighting among girls appeared in *Ophelia Speaks*, an anthology of girls' voices published in 1999.[2] There was one essay on suicide. As she noted in the introduction, editor Sara Shandler had sent out a widespread call for essays from teen girls, saying, in part:

> Your contributions may focus on different aspects of your pre-adult existence. Possible subjects include:
>
> Body image or eating disorders
>
> Romantic relationships
>
> Friendships
>
> Drug experimentation or abuse
>
> Relationships with parents and siblings
>
> Death
>
> Depression
>
> Sexual preferences
>
> Sexual abuse
>
> Religious faith
>
> Socioeconomic, cultural and racial issues
>
> Why you are proud to be a female

Entries on sexual abuse and rape, friends dying in car crashes, and other topics were published, but nothing about girls fighting. Perhaps it is demographics, those writing essays in response to the request may have been less likely to live or go to school where violence among girls is most frequent, poor urban communities. Perhaps in selecting essays the publishers didn't think girls' fighting was mainstream enough. We don't know. We have a strong suspicion

that essays published today would include episodes of girls fighting—
but maybe not. Maybe girls' violence is still not visible enough
yet. Maybe those writing the essays are still not affected by it—yet.

Both of us work in prevention. In order to prevent something,
society must be ahead of the curve. Now is the time to start preventing girls' violence. Let's not wait until it spreads. The best advice
is found in an African proverb: *When is the best time to plant a tree?*
Twenty years ago. When is the next best time to plant a tree? Now!

Many researchers downplay the increase in girls' violence. They
point out that boys are still responsible for most of the violence or
that the most serious violence, homicide, is still mainly the purview
of boys. Some say that police are just tougher on crime and are
arresting girls for behavior that used to be ignored. These excuses
don't hold water. Girls are committing significantly more acts of
violence than they did even one generation ago. The episodes are
not only more frequent but they are also more serious, thus resulting in arrests and incarceration. We fear the more deadly consequences ahead as girls predictably increase their use of weapons,
particularly guns, in altercations.

Even though girls' physical violence has not received the same
professional attention that girls' bullying, backstabbing, and
cliques have, there are no legitimate ways to discount what is happening with girls. Parents must deal with the fact that physical violence among girls is a significant problem for some communities
and on the horizon for others. Now is the time to focus on prevention. Girls in poor urban neighborhoods across the United States
are fighting, like boys. Given the patterns we have seen, we expect
it to get worse before it gets better. We expect it to spread. Mean
girls will become meaner girls, and just as the first wave of boys'
violence broke through class and geographical boundaries, we
expect girls' fighting to do the same. Why wouldn't it? Although
boys commit more of the violence, although more stringent school
expulsion guidelines such as zero tolerance and stiffer sentences are
causing girls to be arrested more, these two facts do not explain
away girls' violence. Accepting the changes in girls' behavior is the

first step in being able to do something about it. It seems to be just a matter of time.

Blaming the Victims?

Traditionally, girls and women are portrayed and viewed as the "innocent" victims of male violence. Until recently, much movie violence involving girls and women depicted scenes of stranger-perpetrated violence (usually inflicted on a middle-class white victim) that had to be avenged by the male hero. A few movies have treated issues of domestic violence or child abuse. They too represent innocent victims. It is difficult to raise the issue of girls fighting without also arousing images of girls fighting back in self-defense, to which some retort, "finally."

It is more difficult to discuss girls and women as the aggressors, the perpetrators, the criminals, without some worry about "blaming the victim." Girls and women have been put down so long that it feels good to see them rise up in self-defense. Certainly some of girls' violence is self-defense, as is the case among boys. But we find the change in girls' methods of self-defense (from internalized responses such as running away and suicide attempts to violent externalization) worrisome as well. It is a warning to society of the level of danger that may be ahead. If girls begin to behave as violently as boys, even in self-defense, society will most definitely suffer.

Some researchers, in an effort to avoid blaming the victim or to remain true to feminist theory, find many reasons to dismiss the violence perpetrated by girls. They say it isn't as bad as boys' violence. We say true. They say girls haven't really changed much; society is just harsher with punishment now. We say partially true, but this doesn't discount what girls are doing. They say maybe it's a good thing that girls are finally defending themselves and outwardly expressing their anger rather than being passive-aggressive or internalizing. We say no. That kind of outward expression of anger, more typical of boys and men, is a problem. Boys and men should not be the model for handling anger. The skills of self-defense include prevention, negotiation, empathy, and conflict resolution, not just fighting back; this is a lesson for boys and girls, men and women. Handling anger in productive ways requires nonviolent conflict resolution skills. These are skills that must be taught, practiced, and admired and made popular.

Our mission is not to blame girls and women or add to the gender injustice in society. Our mission in writing this book is to use society's fear of the unthinkable (girls as violent as boys) coupled with the knowledge that the unthinkable is looking more possible to fuel violence prevention in America. Now more than ever, it should be clear that it matters what we show to our children, what we say to them, and what we admire. We can and must socialize our children differently. Violence is not okay for boys and it is not okay for girls.

Playground Images

Most older adults have images of disputes on school grounds as petty arguments between girls and physical fights (spats) between boys. In the past boys would fight but rarely if ever use weapons, and girls rarely if ever fought. It was even rarer for a girl to be arrested for a violent offense.

The first few times middle school principals and police told us about girls fighting, we were both caught off guard. At that time, fighting among girls at school was definitely unusual. Although most of our work had been gender neutral, it was clearly geared toward those most involved in the epidemic, boys and young men. Over time it became more frequent to have a school counselor, a parent, or concerned citizen ask Ellen's question, "What should I make of a girl who is fighting like the boys?" Eventually, we came to realize and acknowledge what was happening. We came to understand the need to incorporate girls into our efforts, and not just as bystanders and victims.

We have heard both concern for the safety of the school (as is the case with any fighting) and a worsening sense of ill ease and fear about what might be going on in the world to cause girls to demonstrate the worst and most destructive behaviors of boys. Some have wanted to know if it is even genetically or biologically possible for girls to become as violent as boys. They have expressed fear of not being able to control this new wave of violence and a deep-seated angst that our society will go to "hell in a handbasket" if girls continue to behave as badly as boys. Their fear has in some ways epitomized a prevailing societal belief that girls' extra X chromosome will buffer the many toxins we throw at our girl children—that society can rely on producing nurturing and caring girls who will turn into nurturing and caring mothers and who will hold family and society together regardless of what we throw at them. Girls are proving these beliefs wrong.

Most recently, more and more parents and community leaders are echoing what we have been hearing from school personnel. Interestingly, youths themselves were probably the first to raise concerns—but adults didn't seem to listen, as is usual.

Socializing Boys More Like Girls

Can media and today's culture destroy what seems so basic, so inherent, so natural, and so genetic even? The answer is a resounding yes! This new violent behavior exhibited by girls is shedding more light on the nature versus nurture argument. As girls are being exposed to some of the same violent images, role models (*sheroes*), and social expectations as boys have absorbed over the years, they are now responding with more aggressive and violent behavior. It is as simple as that. They are learning to be violent, just as boys have over the centuries. Girls have moved past empowerment and self-defense. They are now initiating violence to deal with conflict, express anger, display power, and get what they want—just like the boys. (The statistics in Chapter Three confirm this climb in violence.)

Well over a decade ago, psychologist and researcher Leonard Eron stated that if America is to truly reduce youth violence, boys must be socialized more like girls have traditionally been socialized.[3]

Instead, over the ensuing years, we as a society have done the opposite, socializing our girls like boys. Now our girls are demonstrating the violent behavior of boys. If parents ever had any doubt about the impact of cultural values and the media on their children, then the past decade of increased fighting among girls answers that—and pretty clearly too! Girls are not genetically protected from the violent junk in the media and toxic cultural influences. Girls may be resilient to violence, but they are obviously not immune to it.

Not Just an Urban Problem

Deborah was at a fancy country club in a small Midwestern town to speak on violence several years ago, when a mother (one of the Junior League hosts for the event) shared her recent humiliation. A girl in her son's school had beaten up her son, and everyone in this small town seemed to be talking badly about him because he didn't fight back. It had gotten so bad that his girlfriend's family demanded that she break off their relationship because, they said, something must be wrong with him. All because he didn't fight back and was beaten up by a girl. This embarrassed and harassed mother actually felt that her son had done the right thing. She was proud of him but also quite disturbed by the lack of support throughout the community for his actions. Even school personnel were not acknowledging his choice of nonviolence as positive, and in fact, there was an outright celebration of the girl's violent putdown of her son.

That girls are capable of the same or even greater levels of viciousness and violence as boys is a fact many find surprising. Aren't girls genetically hardwired to be nice? How can this be happening? What can we do to stop it before it reaches greater numbers?

The Differences Between Girls' Violence and Boys' Violence

In addition to occurring at significantly lower rates, girls' violence differs from boys' in other ways. Violent crimes committed by girls are less likely to be committed with weapons. When girls do use weapons, they are much more likely than boys to use knives rather than guns.

Girls are more likely than boys to be involved in fights with friends and family—stranger violence is still pretty much a "boy thing" for now, especially stranger homicide. When a girl or young woman commits a murder, it is more likely to take place in the context of an argument among family or friends than to involve a stranger or another crime (burglary or drug dealing, for example).[4]

However, there is also evidence that a girl may turn to violence for some of the same reasons a boy does—to prove she is not a wimp, to build a reputation and avoid future victimization, to mark her property (her man), to defend her mother against insults, and for the fun of it. Yes, for the fun and thrill of beating someone up; that is what researcher Cindy Ness discovered in her work in west and northeast Philadelphia.[5]

Are Girls Just Fighting Back? The Myth of Self-Defense

We are often asked, "Are girls just fighting back? Have they been victimized by boys and men so long that they are deciding not to take it anymore?" Traditionally, traumatized girls would run away, attempt suicide, become prostitutes, and use drugs—primarily self-destructive responses to their pain and anger. We posit that girls, through media and cultural shifts, are learning to respond violently, to externalize their hurt and pain. So in some ways the answer to the question is yes, but girls are not fighting back in the way many are thinking of when they ask the question, not in the way shown in *Enough*, the very popular movie starring Jennifer Lopez, in which a battered woman constantly hunted and chased by her former husband makes a decision to train physically and then go after him. At the end of the movie, she does kill the man who would have killed her. But that's Hollywood . . .

In real life it is rare for a battered woman to kill her batterer, and in real life hurt girls continue to hurt themselves more than others. But now they are also physically hurting others, usually other girls and sometimes boys. They occasionally fight boyfriends. They are much less likely to fight strangers—though we expect that this will change with time. As this wave matures, we expect girls' violence to eventually have a pattern similar to boys' violence. So let's look more closely at both the self-defense argument and a related myth.

Not Just Fighting Back. Most of the violence among girls is directed at other girls. We know this from the stories we are told and from a few studies of school violence. In an odd way it would seem less disconcerting if girls where just fighting back—if they were somehow "justified" in the violence they enact—if it were somehow "explainable" or "understandable." The truth is, their violence is already very similar to the violence of boys. And that should make society (parents, researchers, and experts included) uncomfortable.

The risk factors and reasons for girls' violence are similar too. The cycle of violence (exposing children to violence increases their risk for involvement in violence later in life) applies to girls as well as boys. And for girls, just as is the case for boys, fighting is a frightening indication that social and cultural norms (this society's apparent love of violence) and media portrayals of these norms (the glamorization of violence) are the problem. Equating power with violence sets the stage for everyone, *including girls*, to use violence to gain power and control over a situation.

Not Cattiness Gone Wild Either. A second common myth is that violence perpetrated by girls is somehow innocent or cute: cattiness gone wild. A 2002 *New York Times Magazine* cover story, for example, titled "Mean Girls," describes serious cases of mean gossip, exclusion of unpopular girls, and overall cattiness in private school settings.[6] The article also mentions *Queen Bees and Wannabes*[7] and *Odd Girl Out*,[8] two among a group of recent books on the ways girls are mean to each other and occasionally to boys.

Odd Girl Out, published in 2002, was written by a young woman who in high school was bullied and excluded from a clique by another girl, a "queen bee." While in college she learned that other girls had had similar experiences in similar settings—upper- and middle-class schools, mostly private. In her book she describes a "hidden" culture of aggression among girls and advises parents and teachers on ways to help children in those situations. This book, a national best-seller, sets the stage for recognizing the potential girls have for meanness and the many ways in which this meanness is expressed. *Odd Girl Out* also offers a nearly sentimental portrayal of working-class girls and African American girls, whose "mouthiness" and direct assertive style is considered preferable to the mean, indirect, and hidden style of white, middle-class girls. The risk of physical violence as a consequence of the mouthiness and assertiveness is, however, not discussed. Homicide rates are not discussed. It is as if girls and physical violence are assumed not to mix—particularly where white, middle-class girls are concerned. We fear this assumption is unfounded.

The well-received *New York Times* best-seller *Queen Bees and Wannabes,* also published in 2002, describes the inner workings of the lives of American middle-class adolescents. It takes the reader inside "girl world" and "boy world." The author, Rosalind Wiseman, relied on ten years of experience in school-based work in designing and implementing the Empower Program,[9] which presents students, teachers, and parents with options for dealing with the adolescent years. The book and program cover much more than issues of conflict, yet they directly disclose and address the alternative aggression methods used by girls: backbiting, exclusion, bullying, and so on. The discussion of physical violence occurs almost entirely in the chapter titled "Boy World: The Judges and the Judged," with the exception of a discussion of the violence homosexual students have reported receiving at the hands of other boys. As in *Odd Girl Out,* girls and physical violence are not discussed.

Queen Bees and Wannabes was the basis for the recently released movie *Mean Girls.* Despite the serious, threatening, and even injurious nature of the girls' meanness in this film, there is again an implicit denial of actual physical violence and of the potential for it—such fighting is not part of the discussion.

Although both of these books and the Empower Program are helpful to parents and teachers for understanding and responding to girls during their adolescent years, neither acknowledges the potential for physical violence that girls have and are demonstrating. Although acknowledging that girls can be mean and nasty, the authors write as if girls would never do anything like actually fighting.

If readers are not careful to remember the context, these books can be falsely reassuring—girls are mean but in a different way, and not physically violent. There is even the implication that only poor urban girls, who are mostly members of minority groups, are directly aggressive (read *deviant*—or somehow not really feminine) and prone to physical violence. Although this may be a stereotype that is some-what true for now, it is our contention that this image can and prob-ably will change. Just as people who thought violence carried out by boys wouldn't happen in their neighborhoods have had to face the music, society will have to face the music that girls are not genetically protected from using violence. We expect that just as middle-class, suburban white boys have made it clear that they can and will use violence, the same will prove true of middle-class girls.

Women and Violence

In her 2001 book, *Woman's Inhumanity to Woman*,[10] Phyllis Chesler provides a more academic but very readable discussion of the issues of female aggression. She acknowledges up front the involvement of women in physical violence, but her focus is generally on the dif-ferences between men's and women's aggression. Nearly glamoriz-ing the aggression of men, she describes women's aggression as indirect, sneaky, and out-of-control. She puts forth the theory held by some that women have not been trained in violence the way men have and it is this inexperience that leads to any out-of-control quality they may display.

Despite the seriousness of the indirect and hidden behavior described in all the publications discussed here and the connections between verbal, emotional, and physical aggression, the recent, alarmingly violent behavior by girls is not nearly well enough described and addressed. We do not think this physical violence is a different version of the same old thing (female backbiting and cattiness) made more horrific via technology (cell phones and chat rooms). Instead, we think that the emergence of this third wave of violence reflects significant changes in girls' behavior, changes that mean girls now use and experience violence in much the same way as boys do.

Sisters in Crime

Our interpretation of the problem comes closest to that offered by Freda Adler in her 1975 book, *Sisters in Crime*. Adler puts forth the notion that "women involved in violence and criminal activity reflects the same movement as women's involvement in corporate America or other formerly male dominated positions." She goes on to say, "There is a tide in the affairs of women as well as men, and in the last decade it has been sweeping over the barriers which have protected male prerogatives and eroding the traditional differences which once nicely defined the gender roles. The phenomenon of female criminality is but one wave in this rising tide of female assertiveness—a wave which has not yet crested and may even be seeking its level uncomfortably close to the high-water mark set by male violence."[11]

Using data from the twelve years between 1960 and 1972, Adler demonstrates a rise in female crime in every category except aggravated assault and homicide. (The data in Table 3.1 in our next chapter reveal that female crime rates are currently rising in the latter categories too.) Adler also points out that in the early 1900s, the ratio of males' crimes to females' crimes was fifty to one. In 1975, when her book was published, that ratio was five to one, representing a significant increase in female criminality throughout the last century.[12] Things have really changed!

What Does All of This Mean?

However you view the problem, whatever your political persuasion, however you identify racially and culturally, and regardless of where you live and your socioeconomic status, it is clear to us that the changes in girls' behavior should concern you.

We don't think society can or should nostalgically turn back the clock to some earlier time—first, because we agree with the efforts to equalize opportunities for women and, second, because we understand that even if it were desirable, turning back the clock is not possible. What is possible is changing this society's cultural and social norms. The problem is not that girls and women are gaining equal access across society. The problem is that this is a society that glamorizes violence, equates power with violence, and is unskilled at and even dismissive of strategies like compromise, negotiation, forgiveness, and even just being nice. These are unpopular concepts, and children are not encouraged by popular entertainment media (or parents for that matter) to aspire to have them, as our story about the young man who refused to fight back illustrates.

It isn't just that the entertainment media are feminizing the superhero. It's that today's superheroes and the more recently emerging supersheroes almost always and exclusively use violence to solve problems, and enjoy beating up the bad guy to boot. The make-my-day attitude is everywhere.

Where Do We Go from Here?

How do parents and those who care about girls approach this problem? In the remaining three chapters in Part One of this book, we present the information needed to understand the problem and the steps parents and others can take. We present the numbers that define the changing patterns of behavior in Chapter Three. We are not going to overwhelm you with numbers and complicated data, but we believe it is important to see the real statistics and know that the trend we have been discussing is real.

Chapter Four reviews what is known about the factors that contribute to the risk of involvement in violence and the factors that support resiliency or protection from violence. This information can help adults figure out where to place their energy and resources, especially parents who are struggling to figure out what they can do for their daughters. Chapter Five offers our interpretation of the changes in girls' behavior. Why girls? Why now? What has changed in the environment and culture that has pushed girls into such a destructive and frightening situation?

The chapters in Part Two directly address what parents, teachers, and communities can do. We remain hopeful about prevention because we have seen it in action and we know it can work. There is much that can and must be done.

Chapter Three

Facts and Figures

Mark's birthday party was a highly anticipated event. Angela, his girlfriend, was hosting the party at the hottest new club in Philadelphia. She used her connections to reserve a table. She bought a great birthday cake and a wonderful dress to wear. One of her friends from college, Fran, was flying in from New York. Rachel and Christy, two college friends who had moved to Philadelphia right after graduation, were coming as well. This would be the first time the group of four had been together since a homecoming trip a year ago.

Angela would start graduate school at Temple University in one month. She had just moved to Philadelphia to settle in. She was living in a great part of the city. Populated with students, young professionals, first-time homeowners, and the occasional wino, her neighborhood was one of the most sought after in the city. The club was within walking distance of her house, but they wouldn't walk tonight; they would be dressed to kill and they would have many things to carry.

Mark invited three of his good friends from high school, John, Bill, and Rebecca, Bill's high school girlfriend. For a while now, Angela and Mark had felt that Bill and Christy should meet; they had the same good looks and vivacious personalities and many of the same interests. Christy really seemed to be Bill's type. She was always attracted to the great-looking guys, and Bill was just that! This was the night they were going to meet.

The presence of Rebecca, a former girlfriend, wouldn't be a problem, Mark and Bill assured Angela, because the relationship between Rebecca and Bill had been only a high school fling—now they were all just friends.

As planned, Angela's college friends gathered at her apartment to prepare a special dinner and get dressed. They had a great time together preparing the meal and helping each other with last-minute decisions about their outfits. Mark and his friends arrived for dinner, and it was immediately obvious that someone had forgotten to tell Rebecca to dress up. Angela, Rachel, Fran, and Christy were looking fabulous, and Rebecca immediately began to feel insecure.

The college friends made a wonderful meal that the boys couldn't stop complementing. Rebecca was now feeling a bit threatened all the way around. Sensing how she felt, Fran and Rachel both made a special effort to include her in the conversation, but it didn't help. Rebecca didn't really know them, and it appeared as if their friend Christy was flirting with her boyfriend (at least Rebecca was hoping that she and Bill were getting back together—that had seemed to be his plan). John was the only one who could have helped a bit, but he was distracted by his attraction to Fran. John didn't have the time to soothe Rebecca's insecurities, which continued to stew.

As expected, Christy and Bill were hitting it off; Angela and Mark had been right. Their attraction was annoying Rebecca even before they all left Angela's place, and by the time they made it to the club, Rebecca had had it. She kept her cool though and decided to follow Christy to the ladies room and explain to her that Bill was Rebecca's boyfriend. After their ladies room conversation, the flirtations still didn't stop.

Christy asked Bill about his relationship with Rebecca, and he emphasized that they were only friends. The tension between Rebecca and Christy was noticeable. Angela asked Mark about Bill's relationship with Rebecca; again she got the answer "just friends." Christy and Bill continued to flirt. Rebecca continued to tell Christy that Bill was her boyfriend. Bill continued to tell Christy that he and Rebecca were just friends. Despite the tension, which went unnoticed by most of the others, they all had a great time (all except Rebecca). Finally, it was time to go to the next stop, another club.

While they were waiting outside for their cars, a rather sleazy looking, intoxicated man walked up to Christy and asked her for a sexual favor. Christy said no and, without really thinking about it, turned and added, "but that bitch will do it," pointing to Rebecca. Rebecca had had all she could take, and in a flash she walked over and yanked Christy to the ground by her ponytail. Before she realized what was happening, Christy was on the ground looking up at everyone; her head was hurting and she was feeling very much embarrassed.

Some police officers were close by, saw what happened, and came over immediately. As Christy was being helped up, the police asked if she wanted to press charges. She thought about it for a minute, realized the trouble it would cause her friend Angela, and decided not to.

The next day someone suggested they all hang out together. Fortunately, Fran had the foresight to talk Christy into hanging out with her separately. The two of them talked about the night before. Bill, who was hanging out with the others (including Rebecca), called Christy twice to talk. She could hear Rebecca in the background asking who was on the phone. Fran had had enough of this craziness; Bill was cute but proving to be a real jerk. Christy finally agreed.

Trite but true, girls fight other girls over boys or over boy-related conflicts. That is what studies show and what we hear over and over again. Actually, however, the underlying issues are often insecurity, threats, intimidation, and fear—in this way girls are not too different from boys. Recent studies suggest that girls are now fighting to prove a point, get respect, gain a reputation, and for status. They report enjoying a good fight as well—really not too different from boys.

Specific stories about violence, like the one you just read, can illustrate the details of a particular event, but they are limited. The story of what happened in one neighborhood in Philadelphia among a set of friends does not tell you whether similar fights are happening in other places or how often they are happening. Facts and figures from the police and from surveys, although limited in other ways, can round out the picture. A story is just that, one event or episode. In order to present a better picture of what is happening with girls, we will use both stories and numbers. The numbers give a sense of the big picture and the stories give you sample details, a sense of the issues, and early indications of changes or trends.

The story of the fight at Mark's birthday party demonstrates a few important points: (1) many fights are not reported to the police, (2) girls don't often use weapons, and (3) friends play an important role in egging a fight on or helping to squash it. It is pretty clear in this case that subsequent fighting was prevented by Fran's decision to intervene by talking Christy into spending the next day with her, thus avoiding any other confrontations during the weekend. We do think it's unusual for college graduates to be involved in this kind of behavior, though we don't know whether Rebecca herself was a college graduate or had even been to college. In the stories we have heard about college students involved in violence, alcohol is almost always a part of the picture.

Stories aren't enough to make the case we wish to make, so in this chapter we share some of the national data with you. We cover the highlights and provide a few references. If you want more details, you can locate considerable information by searching Internet sites. If you visit a reliable Web site, such as those prepared by governmental agencies (such as the FBI,[1] the National Institute of Justice,[2] and the Centers for Disease Control and Prevention[3]), universities, or reputable national associations, you will know you are getting good information. Even if you only want to know more about the data for your state or city, you will find the Internet useful. (Parents can take note that these sites are also great for finding information for school projects.)

Numbers (particularly in the big national data sets) are often behind the times, slow to show the trends or changes in behavior.

We remember talking with a group of young urban men during a summer program in 1983. We described the most recent CDC data available, which showed that homicide was the leading cause of death for African American men twenty-five to forty-four years old.[4] We told them that we didn't yet know what the figures were for their age group (fifteen to twenty-four years old). They insisted that homicide was in fact the leading cause of death for their age group as well. A month or so later, the CDC published these data; the young men had been correct.

Also, many acts of violence, like the episode between Rebecca and Christy, are not reported anywhere and therefore are not counted in the facts and figures. Even though police officers saw the episode between Rebecca and Christy, they did not make a report because no charges were filed. This reflects what happens with many, many episodes of violence. Fights at school, at home, or among family, friends, and acquaintances on the street are often never reported. Even when there is a serious injury requiring emergency room treatment, no report need be made unless the injury involves a gunshot wound. Police records, the source of the statistics in the national data sets, report only those episodes that are reported as crimes. One study showed that less than a fourth of the violent injuries seen in emergency rooms are reported to the police.[5]

For a decade or more we have been hearing plenty of stories like the one about the near fight and physical violence at Mark's birthday party and the ones related by schoolteachers like Ellen. We turned to the numbers after we kept hearing more and more of these stories about girls' violence from all around the country. We needed to see if any of the national data sets indicated a problem. The numbers confirmed our fears. Not only were school personnel reporting that girls were fighting more, but girls were also getting arrested for violent crimes at all-time high rates as well and national data sets were beginning to show the increase.[6] Facts and figures do not tell the whole story, but when they are coupled with real-life stories from around the country the picture becomes clearer.

Reviewing the Numbers

Nationally, rates of violent crime have been dropping since the mid-1990s, though the preliminary 2003 data indicate the first national increase in murder in almost a decade.[7] Despite this steady national decline, the rates for violent crimes perpetrated by girls and young women rose and generated serious concern, particularly among police and other law enforcement personnel. The rates of violent crime for girls and young women fluctuate in a similar pattern as national rates; however, the long-range trend for female crime is up significantly. We are not optimistic (not with the overall homicide rates appearing to be on their way back up). It is important to remember that the United States has rates of girls' arrests for violent crime that remain quite alarming when compared to rates fifty or even thirty years ago.

Boys and men commit many more acts of violence and crime than girls and young women do. Arrest rates (number of arrests per population count) demonstrate a truth over time and throughout the world; men and boys have committed and continue to commit substantially more acts of violence than their female counterparts do. Nevertheless, in the United States the decade 1985–1995 marked a period when arrests of girls and women increased substantially. Today girls account for 28 percent of the juvenile arrests for violent crime.[8] If girls were carrying out a proportionate share of crimes, they would be 50 percent of those arrested, reflecting that they are 50 percent of the adolescent population. Boys are still committing more crime. Nevertheless, 28 percent represents a significant increase in arrests of girls; it was quite unusual for a girl to be arrested for a violent crime in the past.

This increase in girls' arrest rates becomes even more worrisome when one remembers that the numbers for boys were going down while arrest numbers for girls were going up. Table 3.1 illustrates this alarming trend. Arrests have gone up for girls while going down for boys in three categories of offenses (shown in bold)—aggravated assault, weapons charges, and larceny-theft. Arrests of girls for sim-

Table 3.1.   Changes in Juvenile Arrests Rates by Gender, 1990–1999

	Girls	Boys
Aggravated assault	**Up 57%**	**Down 5%**
Weapons	**Up 44%**	**Down 7%**
Larceny-theft	**Up 6%**	**Down 24%**
Simple assault	Up 93%	Up 35%
Curfew/loitering	Up 139%	Up 103%
Runaways	Down 12%	Down 18%

Source: Data from the U.S. Department of Justice, Office of Juvenile Justice and Delinquency Prevention, "Female Delinquency Cases" (Washington, D.C.: U.S. Justice Department, 2000).

ple assaults almost doubled, which is quite alarming even though boys went up in that category as well. Only in the areas of curfew and loitering infractions and running away did girls' and boys' arrests change in the same direction and to a similar extent.

For those of us involved in prevention, there is no reassurance in the trends we see. Our concern is not eased by that fact that girls are not yet committing crimes and violent acts at the same level as boys are. We take no comfort whatsoever from the idea that the current "get tough on crime era" and "zero tolerance age" has disproportionately affected girls and may explain some of the trends. For those of us interested in prevention, the changes in arrests reflect changes in girls' behavior, and we are alarmed!

More and Younger Girls over Time

In the past it was unusual for a girl to be arrested for a violent crime. The current arrest rates for girls represent a huge increase over rates in the last century. In the early 1900s, 2 percent, or one in fifty, of the juveniles arrested were girls, by 2000 that number was 28 percent. A look at the ratios over time is startling:

1900: 1 in 50 juveniles arrested for all crimes is a girl.

1975: 1 in 5 juveniles arrested for all crimes is a girl.

2000: 1 in 4 juveniles arrested for violent crimes is a girl.

2003: 1 in 3 juveniles arrested for violent crimes is a girl.

The difference in the denominators (all crimes for 1900 and 1975 versus violent crimes for 2000 and 2003), with more specificity occurring later, actually makes the dramatic increase over time even more alarming.

The greatest increases in overall percentages are seen among younger girls. Here the news is particularly bad and seems to parallel the trend toward younger boys' becoming more involved in violent crime. In the year 2000, among the thirteen- to fifteen-year-old juveniles arrested, girls were 26 percent of those arrested for aggravated assault, 34 percent of those arrested for simple assault, and 39 percent of those arrested for larceny-theft. *More than one in every four teens aged thirteen to fifteen who is arrested for aggravated assault is a girl.*[9] This is truly alarming. Today more girls are entering the juvenile justice system because they have committed a violent crime, and they are doing so at younger ages.

Perhaps Girls Haven't Changed: They Are Just Getting Arrested

Are girls really acting more violently, or are police just arresting them now for behavior that was once dealt with differently? Given a zero tolerance approach and a tougher criminal justice system, are girls just getting caught up in new arrest policies? These are important questions to address.

There is evidence suggesting that the criminal justice system is tougher on girls than on boys for certain offenses. And schools are being tougher in general now, with zero tolerance policies and strong enforcement efforts (school police). However, these tougher policies affect both boys and girls and wouldn't explain the numbers going up for girls and down for boys.

With lesser offenses police discretion often determines whether a person is charged with disorderly conduct or simple assault or is arrested at all. For example, in the case of Rebecca's attack on Christy at Mark's birthday, no arrests were made because Christy did not press charges and the police, even though they witnessed the episode, decided not to arrest Rebecca on any other charges. However, with more serious offenses, like aggravated assault, police have less discretion. The figures in Table 3.1 showing that arrests for aggravated assault went up 57 percent for girls and down 5 percent for boys in the 1990s most likely reflect actual behaviors rather than police discretion. Weapons and larceny-theft charges, two other areas where police have less discretion, went up for girls and down for boys. These arrests too are likely to reflect real changes in girls' behaviors.

Police may be less likely to arrest girls if they share the common belief in this society that girls wouldn't get involved in violence. Also, in some settings there are disincentives for police officers to arrest girls. At a national conference of police officers held in Boston in 2004, an officer from Illinois told Deborah that his unit was less likely to arrest girls because the officers would then have to drive almost forty miles to get to the only holding cell available for females; his county leased this space from a nearby county.

It is clear to us that arresting girls for what used to be called *cat fights* and to be generally ignored does not explain the trends.

Homicide

Until recently, both of us used to tell our audiences that the real-life stories coupled with the arrest data indicated an increase in fighting among girls but that the homicide rates did not show an increase—yet. For many that information produced a sense of safety. If there were no deaths, the stories and data just didn't seem that serious.

We used to say and are still saying, at least for now, that guns are pretty much a boy thing. Girls and women are victims of homicides not perpetrators. Homicide is still substantially a boy and man thing, as is using guns. But, here again, things are not precisely as they used to be. Tragically, the numbers of homicides committed by girls and women increased during 1985–1995. Since then the rates have paralleled those of boys, declining and now increasing again. Women and girls rarely kill, and when they do, it is often a family member. Murders of young children are committed by the mother 30 percent of the time, the father 30 percent of the time, and the remaining 40 percent of the time by another male, often someone known to the family.

Girls who commit homicide are far more likely than boys to kill a parent, stepparent, or other family member. Forty-four percent of the adolescent girls arrested for murder in 2003 killed an adult family member (usually a parent) as compared to 14 percent of the adolescent boys arrested for murder.

The FBI's Most Wanted list is of interest in the evolution of criminal and violent behavior in girls and women.[10] The list was begun in 1950, but a woman did not appear on the list until 1968. From 1973 through 1998, seven women have been on this list, with as many as five appearing at once. In many ways this pattern too indicates that girls are beginning to show up in a new role, a new behavior—as the ones doing the killing.

Other Characteristics of Girls' Violence

For school fights, simple assaults, aggravated assaults, and homicides there are differences between girls' and boys' criminal activity. Girls and young women are more likely to fight other females. They are less likely to use a firearm than boys and men. When they use a weapon, it is more likely to be a knife than a firearm.[11] Girls and women are more likely than boys and men to fight a family member, friend, or acquaintance than a stranger and more likely to fight as a result of an argument. A perpetrator of violence who uses a gun against a stranger is much, much more likely to be male—at least for now. Like their male counterparts, females committing violent crimes are under the influence of alcohol or other drugs more often than not.

What Do Girls Report?

Since 1991, this nation's lead agency for public health research, the Centers for Disease Control and Prevention (CDC), as part of its Youth Risk Behavior Surveillance System (YRBSS), has conducted a large, biannual health risk behavior survey of high school students across the country. This survey provides some reliable and comparable data on risks for violence, despite a notable limitation—only in-school teens are included. From its beginnings, the survey has routinely asked about weapon carrying. In 1993, questions on fighting behavior were included for the first time, in an effort to follow trends in violence in more depth. In the last few years, some questions on victimization were added as well. This rich data set is accessible on-line.[12] In addition to collecting national data, the YRBSS has analyzed teen responses at the community level to look at some state-, county-, and city-specific trends. We encourage all to visit the YRBSS site. (If you don't have the site address handy, just use Google to search for "YRBSS.") If your state or local community has participated in one of the narrower studies, that information will help you to see the specifics of what is happening in your own and your children's environment.

Boys have consistently reported more fighting and more weapon carrying than girls. However, when one looks at changes and trends, girls responding to the 1995 survey generally reported an increase in both of these behaviors, whereas boys generally reported no increase or even a decline. Rates of self-report of fighting and weapon carrying declined for both boys and girls on the 1999 survey. This is likely a reflection of increasing tougher school policies that exclude higher-risk students from the classroom via suspension and expulsion.

Although supplying useful information about trends in self-reported behaviors, teens' responses to questions on surveys about violence and weapon carrying do not necessarily reflect their actual behavior. Their responses are limited by what they remember or want to portray. However, arrest data, while affected by changes in police policies, do reflect actual behavior better than surveys. Arrest data show more alarming trends for girls than self-reported data from surveys. Also, remember that girls who commit acts of violence are more likely to be absent or excluded from school—another reason surveys may underestimate actual fighting behavior.

Weapon Carrying.   In the 1991 YRBSS survey and each survey since then, students were asked, "Have you carried a weapon such as a gun, knife, or other weapon on one or more of the past 30 days?" In 1991, 41 percent of the boys and 11 percent of the girls answered yes. Both these figures have declined fairly steadily over the years, and in 2003, 27 percent of the boys and 7 percent of the girls answered yes. In 1993, several questions about violence and weapon carrying were added to the survey, specifically weapon carrying to school. In 1993, 18 percent of the boys and 5 percent of the girls reported carrying a weapon to school in the last thirty days. In 2003, that number declined to 9 percent for boys and 3 percent for girls.

Needless to say, when students are asked specifically about guns, the numbers for both girls and boys are much less than for any other weapon. Of course *any* gun carrying among high school students, particularly to school, is alarming. In 1993, 14 percent of the boys and 2 percent of the girls reported carrying a gun in the last thirty days; by 2003, the number for boys dropped to 10 percent and remained at about 2 percent for girls. The peak year for boys was 1993 and for girls it was 1995 (at 2.5 percent).

Fighting.   Since 1993, the YRBSS survey has asked students about fighting on and off school property. Again, the number of girls reporting fighting is less than the number of boys but nevertheless disturbing. The peak year for girls and boys was 1993, with

51 percent of the boys and 32 percent of the girls reporting a fight within the last twelve months. By 2003, those percentages had dropped to 40 percent of the boys and 25 percent of the girls.

Fighting at school is reported as getting into at least one fight at school in the previous twelve months. The peak year was again 1993 for boys but much later for girls, 1999. In 1993, 24 percent of the boys and 9 percent of the girls reported fighting at school. In 1999, the number for boys dropped to 20 percent and for girls it rose to 10 percent. In 2003, boys declined to 17 percent and girls to 8 percent. The lowest year for girls was 2001, with 7 percent reporting a fight at school in the previous twelve months.

While YRBSS data are more reassuring than arrest data, we are by no means reassured considering the numerous stories we have been told for over a decade, in combination with (1) alarming arrest rates for girls, (2) dimishing gender gaps for almost every area of endeavor, and (3) the important role of socialization and cultural values on children's behavior. We are convinced that America is facing a third wave of the youth violence epidemic.

More Information Would Be Helpful

The United States does not have a national violence or injury registry like the extensive one maintained for automobile crashes. This prohibits policymakers and concerned citizens from seeing changes and warning signs earlier. For example, it would be helpful to know how many people are seen in hospital emergency rooms for violent injury and death. Hospitals are mandated to report gunshot wounds to the police, and medical examiners are required to report any suspicious deaths as well. However, no one is required to report knife injuries, injuries from fights, or even nonviolent injuries and deaths (drownings, falls from windows in high-rise buildings, and so forth) for that matter. The information available from the police about gunshot injuries and homicides is reasonably reliable, but we know that police assault data grossly underestimate the number of assaults.

Despite wanting to know more and to have more information, there are things that we do know and can share. To be perfectly honest, we don't need more data to know that something has changed for girls, and that we need to be concerned. More data could help us understand why the changes have occurred and what we might do, but we are unquestionably convinced that the increases in violent behavior among girls over the past two decades are real and supported by the stories we hear and the data we review. The more recent declines in weapon carrying and self-reported fighting are encouraging, though a bit confusing given the continual rise in arrest rates. Furthermore, the recent rise, albeit small, in women as perpetrators of homicide and the recent rise in homicide rates nationally may suggest that the positive trends we have seen over the past five years may be starting to reverse.

From Facts and Figures to Action

Regardless of who you are or where you live, it is unlikely that your child will be a victim or perpetrator of a homicide. Fortunately, homicide is an unusual event, even here in the United States where homicide numbers are dramatically high when compared to those of other industrialized countries. That does not mean we can all be complacent, as homicide is just the tip of the iceberg of ways violence can harm the lives of children. In addition, things can get worse (and have been worse in the past for boys).

One homicide destroys at least two families (the victim's and the perpetrator's) and often rips apart a whole community. Right now, it is estimated that one in every sixteen Americans has experienced the murder of a loved one (child, sibling, other family member, or a friend). This experience results in significant trauma (similar to posttraumatic stress disorder), protracted grief, medical and mental health problems, and forever living life with the stigma often attached to homicide.[13]

If we thought these high rates of homicide and the recent rise in girl violence were inevitable, then we wouldn't have written this book. What would be the point? This country does not have to accept things the way they are (and the way they are becoming). Homicide and girls' violence are both preventable. In fact, we think that the fact that girls' violence has increased means it can also be decreased. The first two waves of the youth violence epidemic that involved mainly boys started in much the same way, with much the same early warning signs as teachers, parents, and others are now seeing with girls.

Some experts discount the increase in arrest rates for girls because the numbers are still substantially lower than those for boys and these are times of harsher treatment, perhaps even more so for girls. We are not at all reassured and don't think you should be either. We think it is just a matter of time before the numbers begin to equalize, particularly if the current trends continue. Just as girls have closed about every other gap they once faced in this society, they are closing this one.

Preventable violent tragedy occurs in the United States every day, increasingly involving girls and young women as perpetrators. The answer is not to turn back the clocks to a time when girls were girls and men were men. The answer is to read forward and become dedicated to prevention. Especially as parents, we need to be involved. The answer lies in understanding the pressures and influences on children; protecting them from guns; teaching them to handle emotions; teaching them to admire peace, desire conflict resolution skills, and disdain violence; buffering the junk values the media throw at them, and much more.

There is much that parents can do to encourage safe behaviors, prevent and reduce risk among their daughters and other girls in the community, and provide opportunities for girls to build the skills that promote resiliency. There are also important things that teachers and schools can do, especially if communities commit to change and parents play an active role in demanding and promoting these changes. The one thing this country cannot do is do nothing. We all know where that will lead us and our daughters. Our daughters deserve a better path than the one that lies ahead if we do nothing. What can we do? Read on!

Many people easily accepted the epidemic of youth violence in poor, minority urban communities as compelling and real because it fit existing stereotypes. However, accepting the rash of suburban and rural school violence as part of that epidemic was difficult for most. They wanted to dismiss those episodes as isolated, copycat events. It was the Columbine shooting that seemed to make them unable to continue this dismissing attitude. How unfortunate that it took a massacre to force the issue.

Acknowledging that girls are capable of the same kind of violence as boys is even more difficult, for all of us really. Some feminists have trouble with this notion because they see it as bordering on or even contributing to a "blame the victim" interpretation. Other people have trouble accepting girls' violence as something other than the actions of few "deviants" because it challenges their fundamental way of thinking, which has been summed up as "men are from Mars, women are from Venus."

We ourselves have looked at the trends in light of our knowledge and experiences and concluded that the increased rates in girls' arrests for violent crime, including homicide, are a reflection of real changes in girls' behavior. These are not just "status offenses." They are events where violent behavior and physical harm have occurred. We have therefore concluded that girls and women are behaving more violently than in the past and that this behavior is on the increase. The increase in girls' arrests rates combined with the real-life experience of educators, parents, and youth-serving professionals portends real trouble. Structural inequalities within the juvenile justice system, which do exist, do not explain away the increase of female perpetration. In essence, this book is our strong statement that multiple data sets and our experience over the past two decades with youth violence lead us to one conclusion: America is experiencing a third wave in its youth violence epidemic—girls' violence.

Chapter Four

Risk Factors and Protective Factors

Michelle joined a gang because she felt she really had no choice. Her sister was in the gang. Unlike her sister, Michelle chose to take the same initiation as the boys (jumping in), rather than getting rolled in (having sex with all the male members of her gang's brother gang). She wasn't up for that, so she was left with committing a violent crime. Others had done it. She could do it. You didn't really have to kill anybody, but whatever you did, you had to gain the respect of the others.

Michelle chose to rob a liquor store. She carried a gun to make it easy; she wasn't planning to shoot anybody. The person behind the counter didn't cooperate, things got out of hand, and she did shoot. Michelle was arrested a few days later. Someone had ratted her out, probably the girlfriend of the leader of their brother gang, who had never really liked her sister and seemed not to like her. She seemed to think that Michelle was after her boyfriend.

Now Michelle is pregnant and wanting out. It's hard to get her to talk about her family. Her mother's boyfriend (she didn't really know her father) started molesting her when she was ten years old. She ran away at twelve. She was sent to foster care and, for money, had sex with eight foster brothers in five different homes over the next few years. Now she thinks she should have rolled into the gang because she wouldn't be facing a twenty-five-year to life sentence now. Who is going to raise her baby? What was she thinking?

School? Michelle was never really big on school. She remembers not having school supplies in the first grade and not ever knowing the answer in class. She had one friend in first grade, but he just wanted to see in her pants. She let him. She didn't let him see all of the time—but some of time. He let her see in his pants too.

Her father? Not a clue. Actually, that's not true. She does remember her mother introducing her to a lady she said was Michelle's grandmother. The lady moved away after that, and Michelle never saw her again. She thinks her father is in jail for murder. She's not sure though because when she asked her mother where he was, her mother's reply was, "How the f*** should I know?"

She wishes she hadn't shot that lady. Life would be better for her and her baby. Getting out of Ohio had always been her dream. Now she'll probably be old and gray by the time she's finished spending a life sentence here.

Michelle was in one of the highest-risk situations—she faced many *risk factors* and few *protective factors*. Once risk factors begin to accumulate, things can spiral downward quickly. In our book *Murder Is No Accident*,[1] we use a comparison between a slot machine and the lives of children to paint a general picture of how these factor function. Chance determines what images line up in the windows on a slot machine, and in a large way chance determines the risk and protective factors that line up for each child. When there are many risk factors, they line up to create problems. Some risk factors seem to create yet more risks, and this is the way the lives of girls like Michelle begin to spiral downwards. When there are enough protective factors, they can prevent the risks from lining up.

No single risk factor can be identified as the cause of fighting among girls, particularly when an individual case is being dissected. Risk factors come together and act in synergy to create problems. In a situation like Michelle's, confounding and interrelated factors come together and magnify the likelihood of trouble. A girl or young woman will find herself involved in the juvenile justice system because a lot of little things have eventually added up to huge trouble. Often girls begin their criminal careers with status offenses, like running away, and progress through disorderly conduct to arrests for assaults. The risk factors for violence line up to produce a result the way slot machine windows line up. They line up for girls just as they do for boys.

Risks Come in Clusters

Without an adult role model to help her see beyond her immediate environment to a different life, Michelle was left to make dangerous choices from a list full of self-destructive, illegal, and high-risk behaviors: sexual promiscuity, prostitution, selling drugs, joining gangs, and the like. In this way her situation is similar to that of many girls with many risks and few protective factors. For a girl like Michelle to choose a life of high school and college graduation ending in a successful career and no history of incarceration, she requires a vivid imagination, realistic role models, and an extraordinary ability to make and stick with good choices. She has to do this without the guarantee of rewards or success. She literally has to go against all odds.

For example, several recent studies[2] indicate that girls who smoke cigarettes are more likely than nonsmokers to be sexually active as well. Sexually active adolescent girls are more likely than others to drink alcohol as well. With drug use, a gateway effect has been demonstrated—the use of a legal drug (alcohol or cigarettes) precedes the use of marijuana, which can lead to other illegal drug use. Adolescence is a time of risk taking, and most adolescent girls take some risks without serious consequences. Most do not wind up with multiple risk factors spiraling downward. Protective factors, including parental resources, play a huge role in preventing the accumulation of multiple risks and serious consequences. Michelle didn't have that protection.

The balance between risk factors and protective factors may tip the scale toward or away from the likelihood of involvement with violence and other risky behaviors. The metaphor of the slot machine illustrates that factors may line up in either direction. Today risk factors have lined up to create an epidemic of youth violence in America.

The Major Risk Factors

Although more research needs to be done, the risk factors that precede girls' participation in acts of violence are quite similar to those involved in boys' violence. The general risk factors for violence in America cluster into six big categories: (1) gun availability, (2) poverty, (3) alcohol and other drug use, (4) biological factors, (5) witnessing and victimization, and (6) social and cultural influences. With the exception of gun availability, these risk factors for violence apply similarly to girls and boys.

Gun Availability

Gun availability in the United States is a serious concern for most public health professionals because of the role of guns in homicides. Several studies have demonstrated that gun availability increases the risk of homicide, suicide, and assault, despite controlling for other factors. A homicide involving a friend or family member is two to three times more likely in a home with a gun than in a home without one, and the suicide of a family member is four times more likely.[3] American cities have some of the highest homicide rates in the industrialized world, and most of the difference is attributable to gun availability. One study compared rates in Vancouver, British Columbia, and Seattle, Washington—a Canadian and a U.S. city.[4] These cities are very similar in size and demographics and very different in their gun regulations and availability. Seattle had much higher rates of both assault and homicide, and almost all of the difference could be linked to guns. The cities' rates for both assault and homicide involving weapons other than guns (knives and so forth) were very similar, but the rates involving guns were much higher in Seattle. This study sheds light on the question, Do guns kill people, or do people kill people? The presence of a gun seems to influence behavior, resulting in more assaults and homicides than would otherwise happen.

Guns are a significant risk for violence. However, girls and women are not carrying or using guns as much as their male counterparts—not yet.

Poverty

There is a significant and persistent relationship between poverty and all crime. Poor people are more likely to be arrested and are more likely to be victims. There is also, more specifically, a significant and persistent link between poverty and violence. Whether the studies measure unemployment, family income, or broader socioeconomic variables, they consistently show poverty to be a strong risk factor for violence. America's youth violence epidemic that peaked between the mid-1980s and the mid-1990s affected poor urban children, the most vulnerable, first. The second wave, affecting middle-class, suburban, and small-town communities, caught everyone off guard. Economic advantage had been a false reassurance. With the third wave, female violence, poverty is again a risk factor. Poor urban girls are the first affected, but don't be reassured. The drug epidemic is probably the best example of behavioral problems not staying contained in the poor inner city, and given the pattern we have seen with boys' violence, we expect girls' violence to spread as well. Let's not be caught off guard again.

In other words, don't think that your daughter is protected because you have some money. First of all, most young people living in poverty are not violent. Poverty alone is not an adequate explanation for what is going on in most communities. Second, affluent communities are not protected from this issue merely because of their economic resources. Poverty may be a risk factor as affluence may be protective, but there are other considerations that need careful attention.

Alcohol and Other Drug Use

Substance abuse is another significant risk factor for girls. Many girls report being intoxicated while committing criminal acts. As is the case with boys, involvement with illegal drugs seems to propel young women toward deeper involvement in crime.

The American Correctional Association's study of state training schools for girls in the juvenile justice system found that 60 percent of this school population needed substance abuse treatment at intake.[5] This is similar to the findings for boys. The study also indicated that almost half of the girls took drugs or drank alcohol as a form of self-medication. Of the girls who were substance dependent, most first started using drugs or alcohol between the ages of twelve and fifteen. Because this is also the age range in which much of the sexual victimization of girls begins, many think this victimization is the cause of the self-medication. These events may then be followed by clique or gang activity, which may then be followed by running away and violence. Michelle's story illustrates the way risk factors come together and increase the risk by compounding situations. Even though alcohol and other drugs were not mentioned in her case, it's a fair bet that she was drinking or using other drugs, or doing both. The presence of any of the risk factors tends to lead to other risk factors, and they seem to pile on, creating greater and greater risk.

As we mentioned earlier, it has been demonstrated that teens who smoke are more likely than nonsmokers to demonstrate other risky behaviors. If you notice your daughter demonstrating one bad behavior, you should respond with extra resources for her, more supervised activities, and creative punishment (see Chapter Six). Don't ignore the behavior, because it may lead to other risky behaviors and a downward spiral. Michelle's case is the extreme. No one stepped in during kindergarten and first grade when she began demonstrating bad behavior. Early intervention might have helped Michelle onto a new path at a point when change was easier and efforts would have had more effect. The further girls get into a bad situation, the deeper they get, the more difficult it becomes to make a turnaround.

Biological Factors

In some situations violence is more likely because of a biological, or organic, problem. Environmental problems like head trauma (injury), witnessing violence, malnutrition, and lead poisoning translate into biological damage that may be permanent. It is important in discussing risk to distinguish *genetic* factors from *biological* factors. A genetic risk is one that is present within a person's basic makeup. There is no evidence that violent behavior is passed on from parent to child via the genes. There is a lot that is not understood about the brain and its function, but it is known that everything from falling in love to having feelings of rage boils down to biology and biochemistry. Even though genes play a role in each person's chemical and biological makeup, the human body is extremely responsive to the environment. For instance, the large bulging muscles of a man who was of average size prior to doing weight lifting are a great example of the body's response to exercise, an environmental activity.

Head trauma and skull fractures have been associated with perpetration of violence. They may increase the risk for violence through causing biological impairment or through the trauma of witnessing violence or being a victim of it. It is not clear what impact fear has on the body, and in the case of a child witnessing the beating of her mother that impact, though poorly understood, must be significant. Stress and chronically high cortical production or extremely high adrenaline levels associated with the *fight-or-flight* response to danger undoubtedly also have some biological impact on the human body.

There are interesting studies of neurotransmitters—serotonin, for example—that seem to show some promise for explaining and maybe even treating impulsivity disorder or other conditions associated with violent behavior. However, a low level of serotonin in a person's brain doesn't necessarily reflect genetics. Perhaps witnessing violence and the fear or grief associated with victimization are factors that can diminish the productions of serotonin. Whether there is any connection between serotonin and the fight-or-flight response to threats, is unclear. The fight-or-flight response is an adrenaline-mediated response to fear and danger that assists a threatened person by supplying additional energy. Everyone has this response when presented with a threat, but how situations are interpreted and what constitutes a threat is learned.

Witnessing and Victimization: The Cycle of Violence

Sexual and physical abuse are well-worn pathways to female delinquency. A federal study found that girls were three to four times more likely to be sexually abused than boys.[6] Another study of 200 girls in California juvenile detention centers identified early childhood victimization among 92 percent of the female inmates.[7] Another study showed that girls who are arrested and have a self-reported history of being abused or victimized are twice as likely to be charged with a violent offense as are other arrested girls.[8] Girls seem to be especially vulnerable to the cycle of violence—in the past taking it out on themselves, now becoming physically violent toward others as well. A history of victimization (abuse or neglect) increases girls' risk for future participation in violence, either as victims or perpetrators. Girls are more likely than boys to be victimized in the home—by a parent, stepparent, or guardian—or by a boyfriend or intimate partner and are more likely to kill a family member when they do murder.

In the past girls and boys responded differently to the trauma in their lives, in large part because of the differences in the way they are socialized. Those girls who were victimized at home often hurt themselves by running away, becoming prostitutes, becoming drug addicted, or displaying a combination of these behaviors. But violence is increasingly a part of the repertoire of the ways girls right the wrongs against them, just as it has always been for boys. Girls still resort to suicide attempts, running away, substance use, sexual promiscuity, and prostitution to deal with their hurt and trauma. Now, acting violently has been added to their list.

Frequently, society's view of those who commit crimes is one-dimensional: they are simply perpetrators who hurt victims and their families. But the picture is infinitely more complex, especially for girls. Unfortunately, very little is known about the relationship between victimization and subsequent perpetration, yet what is known is enough to act on. The vast majority of female offenders are victims, often victims of sexual abuse. Among female delinquents the statistics are even more frightening; approximately 70 percent have a history of sexual abuse, and 90 percent of this abuse occurs prior to girls' fifteenth birthday.[9]

Adolescence is already turbulent as teens try to answer that age-old question, Who am I? while balancing academics, peer relationships, romantic relationships, and family issues. Sexual, physical, or emotional victimization during or just prior to this critical developmental period often results in decreased self-esteem, the inability to trust, academic failure, eating disorders, and teen pregnancy. Young women charged with running away are almost always running away from abusive situations at home. If your daughter's friend shows up on your doorstep, make sure you do everything you can to help, perhaps even taking her in for a while; she may be escaping physical or sexual abuse at home.

Dating Violence. Approximately 10 percent of dating teenagers have experienced some violence in the context of a relationship, and among both teens and adults, between 30 and 40 percent report violence in an intimate relationship. A survey of three high schools, one each from inner-city, suburban, and rural communities, showed that 18 percent of the students reported experiencing some form of physical or sexual violence or both in a dating relationship.[10] Although the percentage of young women reporting dating violence varies depending on the way the questions are asked, what is clear is the reality of dating violence across color, community, and class lines.

Not all of this violence is against girls and women, and not all of the violence is in heterosexual relationships, but the overwhelming majority is both—violence against a female victim that is perpetrated by a male intimate. However, among adolescents, both females and males may engage in dating violence as *abusers*. Recent surveys conducted by the Centers for Disease Control have shown that adolescent males and females report inflicting equal amounts of violence on a dating partner.[11] Needless to say, these findings are highly debated because girls may be more willing to report than boys, and it is clear that boys actually physically injure girls far more often than the other way around. Among adults, men have consistently been shown to underreport and minimize the violence they inflict, whereas women do not.

Teens give various reasons for using violence in a relationship. Young women report engaging in acts of physical violence in a dating relationship for reasons of uncontrolled anger, jealousy, self-defense, or retaliation, whereas young men report their motives as wanting to intimidate, scare, or force their female partner to give them something.

Because of their lack of experience in dating relationships and the normal developmental challenges facing them, adolescent girls are at particular risk for not recognizing and naming the abuse that occurs in their relationships. Helping your daughter learn the difference between expressions of concern that come from love and exercises of control that come with dangerous jealousy is an extremely important part of your job as a parent. This is where other caring adults who are trusted friends can play a role. As an adolescent, your daughter is charged with developing an identity as an individual that is separate from her family identity. Your opinion on boyfriends may be less important to her than others' opinions, so it might be helpful for you to insert a few "trusted others" into her sphere.

When a girl has witnessed family violence or been victimized, she is more vulnerable to misunderstanding the signals given by a boyfriend. Most of these dating relationships start off wonderfully, with her as the center of his attention; she feels valued in a special way. Family and friends may feel that it is a bit too much attention (an important signal for parents). He responds by isolating her to the point where he is the dominant source of her information and feedback. What started as something special, turns controlling and even violent. Parents can help their daughters by making sure there are other trusted adults in their lives. We cannot stress this enough.

Teen pregnancy is also a risk factor for perpetration. As we have seen, the risk factors frequently overlap, creating numerous obstacles for a young woman to overcome. Young women who are experiencing sexual abuse at home are more likely than other young women to become sexually active early. Moreover, if a young woman is also using illegal substances, she may be less likely to use birth control, increasing her chances for becoming pregnant or being infected with a sexually transmitted disease. Forty percent of women in the general population, 60 percent of the women on welfare, and 80 percent of the women incarcerated give histories of sexual and physical violence, usually perpetrated by a male intimate partner, relative, or friend and usually reported before age fifteen.[12] Today girls are responding differently to the pain, anger, and hurt of sexual molestation—rather than turning it inward, they are turning it outward, externalizing it as violent behavior.

Date Rape, Sexual Abuse, and School Threats. Although saying *date rape* may seem to lessen the impact of the crime, date rape is rape. Sexual victimization at an early age consistently appears in the histories of approximately half of girls and women who have been arrested, incarcerated, or involved in episodes of violence. Sexual victimization ranges from repetitious, unwanted sexual advances and coercion by an abuser to frank rape with penetration. It also includes *date rape*, a euphemism for nonconsensual sex between people who are on a date and/or considered to be in a dating relationship. Findings from a 1992 study, using explicit language and a clear definition of rape, have led to the estimate that 683,000 adult women are raped in the United States each year, and young women and older adolescents are at the highest risk.[13]

In recent years the Youth Risk Behavior Surveillance System (which conducts a national high school survey every other year, as discussed in Chapter Three) has asked questions about dating violence and sexual assault. In 1999, 9 percent of the girls and 8 percent of the boys reported being hit, slapped, or physically hurt on purpose by a boyfriend or girlfriend at least once during the past twelve months. In 2001, 10 percent of the girls and 9 percent of the boys reported such dating violence. In 2003, it was reported by 9 percent of both boys and girls. In 2001, 5 percent of boys and 10 percent of girls (twice as many as boys), reported being physically forced at least once to have sexual intercourse when they did not want to. In 2003, both numbers went up, to 6 percent of boys and 12 percent of girls.

Social and Cultural Influences

Parents, teachers, other school personnel, and society at large play a role in the socialization of girls. Social and cultural norms set expectations and parameters. Expectations and parameters determine behavior. Parents know this intuitively; efforts to put children in the best school system, select and monitor a child's friends, move to a safer neighborhood, or make changes in public policy, all reflect an understanding of the ways cultural norms matter.

Ready access to entertainment media of all sorts has made some cultural norms universal, creating the hip-hop generation for example. It is nearly impossible to tease out the relative impacts of parents, peers, schools, other adults, and the entertainment media on an individual girl's behavior. Yet what is clear from many, many studies is the significant roles that peers and the entertainment media play.

The major risks for violence in America—gun availability, poverty, alcohol and other drug use, biological factors, witnessing and victimization, and social and cultural influences can converge on any given situation to create danger, particularly violence. These factors have different levels of influence on different girls and situations, and they can be offset by protective factors. As with boys, both risk factors and protective factors influence girls, and it is the balance between the two that determines the outcome.

Risks and Protective Factors Operate at Multiple Levels

There are factors that put individuals and communities at risk, and there are factors that are protective and promote resiliency. These factors operate at the individual, family, peer, school, and societal levels (displayed as concentric circles in Figure 4.1). We think that the closer to the middle circle a factor operates, the greater its influence. Family is considered the largest influence around the individual child. However, we show the influence of peers as equal to that of family, because that is the case during adolescence. Actually, during the teen years the influence of peers has been shown in many studies to be even greater than that of parents and immediate family. That is why the "R" (reach out to others) in our ART of parenting model is so important. Reaching out to others, especially the parents of your child's friend, can be a lifesaver during those years. (We discuss this in much greater detail in Chapter Seven.)

Poor academic performance, early sexual activity, smoking, and alcohol and other drug use are all risky behaviors that indicate greater risk for other risky behaviors including violence. Of course different children express risks differently, and girls are still overall much less likely to act violently than boys. However, as the statistics presented in Chapter Three demonstrate, girls are displaying aggression and physical violence more and more. If the pattern America experienced with boys and violence holds true for girls and violence (and we think it will), society cannot realistically expect the rise in girls' fighting to remain a characteristic solely of the most vulnerable girls in poor urban communities.

Figure 4.1.   Circles of Influence

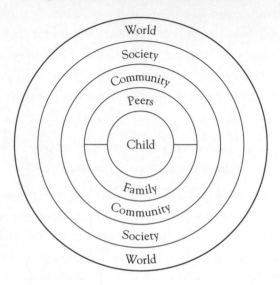

If you are a parent, you should interact regularly with your child and look out for the emergence of any risk factor. An ounce of prevention is truly worth a pound of cure. If you address such things as slumping school performance or smoking marijuana early and creatively (see the suggestions for creative punishment in Chapter Six), you can nip them in the bud and prepare the ground for healthy and engaging activities to distract your daughter from involvement in risky behaviors. We want you to remember that risky behaviors often come in multiples, lead to other risky behaviors, and more often than not have been practiced for a while by the time you become aware of them.

If your child or your child's friend (yes, it is wise to become responsible for your child's friend) displays some of the risk factors, you have to help build her protective factors. Protective factors for teens have a lot to do with having healthy adults around as role models and having some healthy activity at which the teen can excel. Whether it's cheerleading, debate team, track, or serving on the yearbook staff, teens are strongly attracted to group activities with each other and positive activities should be found, even if it means starting one, stopping it, and starting a different one a few weeks later. This is a trial-and-error process, and parents who understand that will avoid investing too much in an activity too early (rent the musical instrument rather than buy it; pay for the minimum number of lessons, not a year's worth). Expect your daughter to change her interests and her activities. This is where you have to be both patient and tenacious, helping her (and her friends) find the right activity.

A Focus on Protection

Unfortunately, we know far less about resiliency than risk. It is easier to study situations that have gone awry than to study factors that have led to nothing bad happening. We do, however, have some understanding of resilient kids from studies of youth and adults who have achieved success even when coming from difficult, high-risk backgrounds. This is as important in creating effective programs as understanding the factors that create risk. Toxic environments exacerbate risks and reduce resiliency. Effective prevention reduces risks and promotes resiliency by creating nurturing environments.

The first and foremost requirement is the presence of a stable, positive, emotional relationship with an adult. Who this adult is— a parent, a relative, a neighbor, a teacher, an outreach worker, a church member, and so on—may not matter; it appears that it is the presence of a nurturing, caring adult that is of great significance to almost every child. The presence of such a relationship promotes resiliency; its absence leaves a child open and vulnerable to negative influences. An evaluation of Big Brothers Big Sisters, for example, demonstrated the efficacy of mentoring programs even in the short range.[14] The evaluation was scientifically strong and showed that within eighteen months of receiving a big brother or big sister the children improved on several outcomes, including better school attendance and delayed onset of experimentation with sex and drugs. This was especially true for girls receiving a big sister.

Building on Success

Above and beyond this crucial factor are several other characteristics that telegraph girls' likelihood of success. Girls who have already experienced success in their lives are likely to continue to be successful and overcome adversity. Although this sounds obvious, it requires that girls be given opportunities to be and feel successful. This isn't always as simple as it seems. It requires that the adults around a child understand her developmental capabilities and expose her to tasks she can master. It also requires that kids who have innate disabilities be given specific opportunities to experience success that may be different from the opportunities other children may need.

Similarly, girls with the skills to thoroughly analyze their environment are able to manage and master that environment more successfully. Society's investment in maximizing the cognitive or intellectual development of girls is essential and has a huge return on investment. This includes reducing exposures that impair intellectual ability (such as lead poisoning) and increasing exposures that enhance development (such as Head Start).

In addition, developmentally, girls are at risk for loss of self-esteem as a result of gender bias and socialization. Carol Gilligan wrote eloquently about this developmental phenomenon in her book *In a Different Voice: Psychological Theory and Women's Development*.[15] Girls feel pressured to give up expressions of their true opinions (or voices) in order to rise to the pedestal of being desirable to boys and socially acceptable. This represents a potential risk for abuse and victimization. Parents and extended families must provide the necessary boosts to a girl's self-esteem throughout adolescence to counter the pressures she encounters to silence her voice.

Girls who have skills to actively handle challenges do better than those who passively react to stress. Imparting skills to parents

so they can teach their daughters active problem solving can promote girls' resilience. Incorporating into early intervention, pre-
school, and school programs curricula that promote active and
proactive behavior to face challenges will also build resilience. All
involved with children have to get past a narrow focus on teaching academic content and what is right and wrong and begin
teaching process as well. Learning how to approach problems and
tasks is as important as learning to read and add.

A Nurturing Environment

Girls do better when they exist in nurturing environments. Feeling
safe, loved, and supported promotes healthy behaviors and constructive coping mechanisms. The manner in which girls are treated
in their homes, their schools, and their communities can greatly influence the kind of teenagers and adults they become. This requires
a greater level of child focus in our communities and, quite frankly,
in our schools and requires that we provide more substantial support to families so they can better nurture their girls.

   None of us are innately or biologically programmed to use violence when angry or facing conflict; we learn to do so, and we teach
our children to do the same. The fight-or-flight response, which is
biological, is designed to protect us from danger. When conflict, in
a context of poor conflict resolution skills, generates escalating
anger and ultimately danger, that is cultural not biological. What is
potentially overwhelming is the strong evidence that this learning
process occurs in many areas of a child's life and at very early ages.
For this reason, having an impact on the learning process involves
addressing many different situations. Parents must understand what
situations and experiences produce resiliency and enhance opportunities for positive learning and what situations do not.

   Ultimately, it is the mix of risk factors and protective factors
that affects the outcomes for individual girls and for communities.
Protective factors are reflected in a child's ability to deal with difficult situations and her sense of self-worth or self-esteem. The role

of parents and family cannot be exaggerated. The presence or absence of family makes a huge difference. In her book *Sex, Power, and the Violent School Girl*, Sibylle Artz reports on her work with six violent schoolgirls during one year. She reinforces the important role of family and the potential family carries to enhance resiliency and protective factors or to produce even greater risks in the lives of children.[16] Similarly, what is striking about the story with which we started this chapter is not just the risks Michelle faced but the absence of protective factors in her life.

Academic Performance

Imagine how Michelle's story might have been different if in first grade, when she did something wrong (like not bringing in her homework), the teacher or another parent had responded by helping her. Perhaps the principal and other teachers could have paid special attention to her at that early age, using creative punishment strategies. For example, rather than punishing Michelle in traditional ways (such as not letting her go on a field trip), they could have *overincluded* her—making sure that she was involved in activities and special events that require parental action or participation. Once a school system realizes that a child isn't getting much of a fair start from a chaotic or inattentive home situation, a surrogate parent could be assigned. That's where you come in. If there is a child in your daughter's class who needs help, maybe you and your family can play a role. It will turn out to be a good thing for that child but may also be a good thing for your child as well.

Several studies have linked early academic failure with the onset of delinquency, and there is some research to support the hypothesis that academic failure is an even more powerful predictor of chronic female delinquency.[17] This means that if a girl is doing well in school, it may go a long way to keep her out of trouble and reduce the chance that she will commit violence. School-based programs are extremely important because they can serve two purposes, improving academic performance and teaching conflict resolution and violence prevention skills.

As is also true for boys, girls with learning disabilities are disproportionately represented in the juvenile justice system: 26 percent of female offenders have learning disabilities. Research also reveals that 78 percent of female juvenile offenders have not completed high school or obtained a GED. Girls are also seven times more likely than boys to drop out of school for family reasons. Twenty-seven percent of girl offenders dropped out of school because they were pregnant and another 20 percent left because they were already parents and needed to care for their children. Academic failure is the most significant risk factor relating to early onset of delinquency, in part because it is associated with many other risk factors (such as early pregnancy and substance use) and because it leads to underemployment and underemployment leads to poverty.[18]

Race and Class

As is the case with young men, young women of color are disproportionately represented in the juvenile justice system. Fifty percent of young women in secure detention facilities are African American, and 13 percent are Hispanic. Seven of every ten cases involving Caucasian girls are dismissed; only three of every ten cases are dismissed for African American girls. African American, Asian, and Latina girls who are poor and addicted are more likely to be incarcerated than Caucasian girls with the same characteristics, who are more likely to be referred to mental health facilities.[19] This is essentially a replication of the already well-described bias against young men of color in the criminal justice system.

In addition to inequalities within the justice system, institutional racism often impedes a young woman of color's efforts to obtain a quality education and employment. Repeated lack of opportunity can create frustration, which increases the possibility that a young woman may engage in destructive activities toward herself and others as a way to vent her frustration. Sometimes, perceived economic necessity can lead girls to commit crimes. The 1990 report issued by the American Correctional Association indicated that 9 percent of the girls surveyed broke the law because of economic pressure.[20] However, employment does not, by itself, alleviate delinquency and without other strategies may exacerbate a problem by providing additional funds to purchase illegal substances. This is clearly a complex situation, and more research is needed to further understand the interplay of these factors. As you can see, one cannot always assume the obvious.

Risk and protective factors are not simple to highlight or understand. It is important for parents to appreciate that it is the balance between the two that is critical. Often those arrested, charged, found guilty, and sentenced are those lacking in protective factors. This is true for girls and boys. An understanding of risk and protective factors can help parents find a way out of difficult situations. We go into more detail on this in Chapter Six. But before we move into the strategies, it is important to answer another question: What risk factors explain girls' dramatic increase in violent behavior?

Chapter Five

Feminization of the Superhero

The risks factors we outlined in Chapter Four have plagued girls and young women for decades. So what has changed? What explains the significant change in girls' behavior over the last few decades? What explains the increase in girls' arrest rates for violent crime at a time when boys' rates were declining?

We think *social and cultural change* explains the change in girls' behavior. We call this change the *feminization of the superhero*. We are specifically describing the changed ways the entertainment media (movies, television, music, and teen magazines) depict girls and women. They are appearing in roles that a male superhero could play with very little change in the script. Today's culture is socializing girls more as boys are socialized (the opposite of what psychologist Leonard Eron has suggested doing, as mentioned in Chapter Two), and girls are now behaving more like boys.

As with all questions about complicated problems, there are no simple answers. In the case of violent behavior, the risk factors come together (like the windows of a slot machine) to create situations where individuals use violence to respond to problems and emotions. The same is true for girls in America. The risk factors have lined up and the behavior has changed.

As we described earlier, the major risk factors for violence are gun availability, poverty, alcohol and other drug use, biological factors, witnessing and victimization, and social and cultural influences. In past centuries, when these risks lined up for girls and for boys, girls reacted differently from boys. Girls seemed to use more self-destructive responses to their trauma and pain than boys did. It was by using alcohol and other drugs, running away, attempting suicide, and turning to prostitution that girls would (and still do) express hurt that was inflicted upon them. For example, consistently, 80 to 90 percent of prostitutes report being raped at early childhood ages, often before age ten. Boys have traditionally externalized their responses to trauma, displaying more fighting, bullying, and acting out.

We think the socialization of children and the cultural influences upon them determine the ways they behave and respond. Much as James Garbarino does in his book *Raising Children in a Socially Toxic Environment*, we conclude that society sets the parameters within which children behave.[1] "Bad" or "acting-out" children in an Amish culture might ride in a friend's car or decorate their buggy with brass rings. "Bad" or "acting-out" children in urban America might serve as the lookout for a drug dealer and in suburban America might sell drugs. We think that the parameters around girls' behavior have changed; their repertoire of responses to problems and pain has expanded to include violence.

Aren't Girls Genetically Protected from Acting Violently?

Society's astonishment and even outright denial of girls' violent behavior suggest an expectation of some sort of genetic protection within girls, as if females' XX chromosomes somehow protect them from the effects of a toxic environment. In the past, female crime was attributed to some sort of deviance in a particular girl or woman, not as behavior all females were capable of committing. In a way surprisingly similar to its assumption that boys' violence would never reach the suburbs or small-town America, our country has ignored the vulnerability of girls exposed to violent female superheroes and images and other risk factors.

In order to try to understand what caused girls' fighting to go up at a time when boys' fighting declined, we decided to explore each risk factor to determine whether one or more had changed for girls and not for boys. We acknowledge that this exploration is a rather straightforward approach to a complicated question; however, it has allowed us to focus in on the most plausible answer. In searching through the risk factors to determine what changed for girls and not boys, we discovered that there is one category that has changed dramatically and differentially for girls and boys—the cultural and socialization factors.

Searching the Risk Factors for an Explanation

Poverty, one of the most consistent and intractable risk factors, does not explain the change in girls' behavior. Girls and boys grow up in the same homes. When poverty rates go up for girls, they go up for boys. Therefore, changes in poverty wouldn't explain girls' rates of violence going up while boys' rates declined.

Gun availability is another risk factor to explore. Yet the presence of guns does not explain the rise of rates of violent crime for girls. First of all, guns are still pretty much a boy thing. Second, children most often get the guns they use from their homes (the homes of parents or friends) or from someone in their neighborhood. Boys and girls live in the same homes and communities and in theory have had the same access to guns over the years. We think that guns remain pretty much a boy thing for continuing socialization and cultural reasons, not some testosterone-based, genetic predisposition to firearm use. We also think that it is just a matter of time (if nothing is done) before girls will begin use guns more frequently. (We hate this projection, but as we look at today's entertainment media and the other trends in youths' violent behavior, this is what we fear.)

Alcohol and other drug use is another risk factor to consider in this effort to explain the increases in girls' arrest rates while boys' rates decreased. The Youth Risk Behavior Surveillance System (YRBSS) we discussed in Chapter Three, a survey of 15,000 high school students that has been conducted every other year since 1991, finds that boys consistently report more alcohol and other drug consumption than girls. However, the rates for boys and girls go up and down together. When girls report higher rates, so do boys. When boys report lower rates, so do girls. Changes in alcohol and other drug use do not seem to explain the differential changes in rates of arrest for girls and boys over the last decade and a half.

Witnessing violence, victimization, and neglect are risk factors that have been shown in both boys and girls to increase the risk for criminal behavior and later arrest. Although the rates of victimization for girls and boys are different (there is more reported victimization of girls, especially sexual abuse), almost all of the victimization occurs in homes with family and extended family or other trusted adults known to the family (neighbors, family friends, clergy) as perpetrators. The same is true for witnessing violence—it is home and community based. Boys and girls are in the same homes and communities. Why would the rates of witnessing or victimization have gone up for girls and not for boys given that they are in the same homes and communities? There is no explanation for the increase in girls' violence in this risk factor.

Media Violence: Nothing Else Explains It

The changes in girls' behavior have followed the last decade and a half of media portrayals of female superheroes beating people up and getting beaten up just as male superheroes do—the feminization of the superhero. The other risk factors for violence—poverty, witnessing and victimization, alcohol and other drug use, and availability of guns—have not changed differentially for boys and girls. *No other changes in a risk factor are as dramatic as the shift toward violence in the images of women and girls in the media that has occurred over the last two decades. No other change is as distinct from boys' risk factors as is the feminization of the superhero.* To those who find solace in the still higher rates of boys' violent crime or who attribute the increase in the rate of girls' arrests to changes in policing practices or who look to self-report data to minimize what is happening with girls, we would pose several questions. Why, as girls and women meet every other mark set by men, professionally, personally, and athletically, would this one be left out? Why would girls not be capable of the same level of violence as boys? That girls' rates of violence aren't as bad as boys' rates doesn't console us. That police are treating girls more harshly than in the past doesn't, for us, explain away the changes we and others have witnessed over the last two decades. That girls in school, along with boys, are now reporting a decline in fighting is not reassuring and does not mitigate what the current arrest rates suggest about violence to come.

We are concerned about the changes girls have shown. We are alarmed by the way the indicators line up—stories from teachers, the experiences related by girls, the concerns of parents, the arrest rates for violent crime, and what we have observed with the first and second waves of the youth violence epidemic. We are concerned not only because these add up to more violent behavior from girls but also because we think arresting girls at these higher rates may in fact increase girls' chances of adopting a criminal lifestyle.

Is the Women's Liberation Movement to Blame?

We are often asked if the women's liberation movement and women's equality are to blame. People ask: "Is it that mothers are in the workforce and no longer at home?" or, "Is it that girls are now raised to be equal to boys and do whatever boys do?" Our answer is that the problem is not equalization of opportunity or gender equality. *The problem is that in this society violence equals power; violence is admired and glamorized. It is the supersheroes' successful solution for a problem—the ultimate strategy.* Everyone in a society will aspire to attain the ultimate level of power, even if it is typically portrayed as an option for only one group. Equality and the desire for equal treatment are not the problem. Belief in the ultimate power of violence is.

Deborah once attended a church service in Detroit where the minister referred to the love of violence as a religion, with rituals, celebrations, tools of the trade, mythology, and a significant following. It is an interesting analogy that explains some of the enjoyment many get from watching violent, horrific responses to revenge. Whether you consider it a religion or an addiction (another way that love of violence is described) this society's admiration and adoration of violence is part of the problem.

Not only is women's liberation not to blame but, we believe, gender equality could become part of the solution. If we in this society socialized girls *and* boys more as we used to socialize girls, as nurturers, problem solvers, responsible for relationships, and so forth, we would see less violence among boys and girls. Perhaps the decline in boys' violence reflects some success in the school-based efforts to build conflict resolution skills. We think Leonard Eron was right when he suggested that we should socialize our boys more like we socialize our girls to reduce violence. Instead, this society has done the opposite.

Does Television Have a Greater Effect on Boys?

Boys have generally been thought to be more adversely affected by television violence because violent behavior usually has been exhibited by male characters. Many researchers in this area have given more attention to boys because of the differences in effects according to gender. Those who have studied girls have shown that girls are also adversely affected by television, although in different ways than boys are.

A 1986 study that combined the results of multiple studies indicated that the effect of aggressive role models and violence on television is significant for girls but also found that it had to be measured differently. At that time, of course, female characters on television were not as aggressive and violent as male characters were.[2] At that time, girls who were heavy viewers of television violence did show a tendency toward aggressiveness, but they did not display aggressive behavior or attitudes in the same way as boys did. Girls showed more subtle forms of antisocial behavior, such as anxiety, irritability, and impatience. Now that female characters are playing the same violent roles as male characters, we expect the impact on girls is similar to the impact on boys. Why would it be different? Girls are showing us the impact already.

"Our models can beat up your models," read the 1999 caption on a billboard advertising Levi's jeans. Above the caption stood a group of young men dressed and positioned to look tough, ready for a fight—a gang. Lest you think girls were being left out, postcards with a Marilyn Monroe–like model in a tough, challenging pose above the same caption were being given away at clubs and hair salons. Clearly, the company wanted to sell jeans by associating wearing its jeans with being tough and strong. The primary audience for this campaign was children and youth.

There is no escaping the impact of a toxic environment even though some resourceful families are able to accumulate protective factors to balance the environmental risks that many children face. The rise in girls who are using violence to respond to situations forces an appreciation of the role of environment and culture. America's toxic environment for children has been well described by James Garbarino in *Lost Boys*,[3] Sissela Bok in *Mayhem: Violence as Public Entertainment*,[4] and many others. Whereas traumatized girls would once resort to self-destructive behaviors such as running away, drug abuse, prostitution, and the like, violence in the guise of entertainment appears to have expanded their options to acts of violence against others. What other explanation is there?

The toxic environment both sets the stage for episodes of violence and perpetuates the cycle of violence—fear, isolation, and meanness and ultimately more violence, more fear, more isolation, and even greater meanness. Breaking the cycle for vulnerable children is difficult but possible. The longer the cycle is in place, however, the more difficult and expensive it is to break.

Girls Are Not Really That Different

Although society's astonishment suggests a belief that girls are somehow inherently protected from the effects of a toxic environment,[5] girls are like boys in that they are the product of socialization and environment. Girls experience an interplay between biology and environment during each developmental phase, just as boys do. They experience long-term effects of trauma, and they go through similar stages of adolescent development and conflict.

We have taken an approach to understanding what is happening that involves going through each of the major risk factors and trying to understand what changed for girls that didn't change for boys and that has led us to the conclusion that the factor that has changed is the media portrayal of women. More and more frequently, women are depicted committing acts of violence that are treated as being admirable. In the 1991 movie *Thelma and Louise*, Susan Sarandon and Geena Davis avenged their poor treatment at the hands of men by shooting them or setting them on fire. In the movie *Set It Off*, four women dissatisfied with their lives, led by a character played by Queen Latifah, commit various violent and illegal acts and are portrayed as heroes. On TV we all see *Xena: Warrior Princess*. In print ads we see women carrying handguns that are "sleek and beautiful" and "fit easily into your purse," and those attempts to sell blue jeans with the line "our models can beat up your models."

Perhaps more disturbing is the trend in children's programming. Cartoons, already the most violent genre on TV, have expanded their violence repertoire to include a small but growing number of violent female characters. The list includes the Pink Power Ranger, using violence to bring about justice, and Angelica, the spoiled and short-tempered Rug Rat. More and more frequently, we hear women musicians glorifying and justifying violence. Hip-hopper Eve sings about killing an abusive man, and Courtney Love's songs are filled with violent images. It is difficult to evaluate the impact of these media messages on young people. However, research by Albert Bandura clearly shows that children and adults alike learn through example.[6] Thus, seeing violence glorified as admirable and without consequences, particularly when the perpetrator is someone similar to oneself, increases the chances that the child viewer will see violence as acceptable.

The Power Rangers are the first example we can remember of girls (the rangers in the pink, yellow, and light-blue suits) beating up and getting beaten up in the name of solving a problem, just like the boys. Fifteen years later this country has an epidemic of girls as violent perpetrators. Obviously, we don't blame this solely on the Power Rangers, yet the only risk factor that seems to have changed for girls over the last two decades and not for boys is this feminization of the violent superhero. The Power Rangers may have been among the first, but they have been followed by an ever-increasing number of violent female heroes.

A New Social Norm: Girls Fight Back Too

Why should girls take it any more than boys do? With guns as the great power equalizers, girls are able to defend themselves, seek revenge, and right wrongs just as boys are expected to do. Is this an unintended consequence of the women's liberation movement and the move to equalize the roles for men and women? Is the phenomenon of "girls fighting back" a bad thing or a good thing? We reserve judgment on this but do feel strongly that when a person decides to defend him- or herself in a society where violence is the admired, glamorized, and most frequently portrayed problem solver, the result is likely to be violence. We all certainly want girls to feel and be empowered to defend themselves, to seek equality, and to achieve success on levels equal to boys' success. But do we want them to fall into the same deep hole we have already dug for boys? On the contrary, we want their success to lead us down a different path while we try to fix the situation we have created for boys.

From Victim to Perpetrator

Even though the link between victimization and further perpetration of violence has been poorly explored in girls, the studies that have been conducted indicate a relationship similar to the one found with boys. Cathy Spatz Widom's work clearly demonstrates the higher risk abused and neglected children have for arrests for violence.[7] This effect was true for both boys and girls. The connection between hurt children who then hurt other children is a strong and persistent one. One study of female adolescents incarcerated in juvenile facilities showed that 62 percent had been physically abused and 30 percent said that the abuse began between the ages of five and nine.[8]

Girls' attitudes about violence and using violence have not really been measured over time, but the more recent snapshots are revealing. The Center for Women Policy Studies found that girls who had been physically abused were twice as likely as girls who had not to view violence as "always okay when someone threatens you." The same survey, not surprisingly, indicated that 82 percent of the girls said they felt justified in being violent if someone tried to force them to have sex. However, quite striking were the 23 percent who said that violence was justified if someone started a "bad rumor" about them.[9]

Although girls and boys are different, the increase in girls' violence indicates two things: girls are not as different biologically from boys as many people expect, and society actually creates most of the behavioral differences, by socialization. It seems that the female capacity to give birth to children does not mitigate any natural capacity for violent behavior. It is fairly well accepted that girls and women have the capacity for defensive violent behavior (for example, responding to threats to their children); however, the kind of predatory and offensive violent behavior that resembles the violent behavior of boys challenges the reigning social theories to explain violence and gender.

Handling Anger Like a Man

Boys and men should not be role models for handling anger and aggression, despite the numerous suggestions in the recent "mean girl" literature that girls need to be direct; more willing to fight it out; able to confront, win or lose, and let it go; and better able to get over the anger, like boys. In addition to Hollywood's prescribing "male" behavior for female superheroes, several contemporary authors have suggested that a "male" script would somehow be better for girls to follow.

Phyllis Chesler, in the introduction to the Plume edition of her book *Woman's Inhumanity to Woman*,[10] lists nine steps women might take to deal with women's unacknowledged aggression. One step, "learn to express your anger: rules of engagement," sets men up as the model: "Perhaps here is where women can learn some of the rules of engagement from men about how to fight fairly and then, win or lose, move on, befriend our opponents, or at least quit holding a grudge." Although it is clear from the full context and the other steps that Chesler is not prescribing violent behavior, she is clearly holding men up as a model. She is prescribing the cold, detached, fighting manner of boys and men (who are responsible for most of the serious violence) as better than the protracted, entangled, ongoing, indirect manner of female aggression. This boys will be boys, first they fight and then they become best friends, junk mythology is a large factor in America's youth violence epidemic, particularly when you throw in a few weapons. Whether it's interpersonal or international, violence is rarely the contained, controlled problem solver that it is frequently portrayed as being in society as a whole. And Chesler isn't alone in idealizing and preferring boys' aggression to that of girls.

Fortunately, this sentiment is countered successfully in other writings. Remember what Leonard Eron said: "If we want to reduce violence we must socialize our boys more like our girls."[11] We in this society have done the opposite, and history suggests that we will continue to do so in the near future, at least until a pair of blond, white, middle-class, suburban girls who failed to make the cheer-leading squad actually pull the school fire alarm and shoot at their classmates as they leave the building. Unbelievable isn't it—unless you consider how unbelievable that scenario seemed for boys until it happened.

Things have changed, and we are continuing to move girls in a dangerous direction. New role models, social expectations, and cultural messages have led to new responses including physical aggression, weapon carrying, violent crime–related activity, and empowerment displayed through aggression (presenting a dilemma for those who would be both nonvictim and nonviolent). We are sending girls down the same path that we have been sending boys down for far longer.

Again, it is our position that the problem is not equalization of the roles between girls and boys. The problem is that we live in a society that believes in violence. We in this society admire and glamorize violence and are now inundating girls with images of vio-lent female superheroes to emulate.

Consider the movies *Kill Bill*, volumes 1 and 2, spellbinding, bloody, horrible, revenge flicks, with beautiful women fighting to the death. After a vicious fight in which one female character is killed, another female character says to the daughter who has just witnessed the murder of her mother something like, "I'm sorry you had to see this, but what has to happen has to happen." What im-pact could this kind of solve-your-problems-violently-and-without-consequences movie have on girls or even on young adult women (girls aren't, technically, supposed to see it)? How long will that impact take?

Assume for a minute that you don't agree; assume that this kind of movie won't lead to changes in girls' behavior and won't shift the paradigm toward girls' becoming more and more physically violent. How then would you explain the already existing changes in girls' fighting behavior? What do you think the impact of this kind of movie is?

In reality, even the traditional distinct styles of socializing girls and boys are both inadequate as violence prevention. We in this society have taught boys to be the aggressor and girls to be the victim; neither is what we want. Yet our well-intentioned efforts to promote gender equality have resulted in more aggressive girls. We are now teaching our girls to be the aggressor—nonvictim but very violent.

Learning to Enjoy Violence

Laugh tracks on cartoons teach children that violence is funny. Children also learn to laugh at violence from their peers. Together, these experiences teach children to perceive violence as entertaining. The more they watch, the more they learn this. This begins the development of a "taste" for violence, much as one develops a taste for wine. The industry lays a good foundation for a lifetime of violent entertainment without consequences, pain, death, or sorrow. This is the foundation for the so-called natural appetite for violence.

As they learn to laugh at violence, over time children also become numb to their natural empathy for victims of violence. Many children cry and are very sad when they initially learn that animals are slaughtered for food. Many parents tell stories of children crying and having to be consoled when first witnessing a lobster dropped into boiling water or having their first experience with hunting and being expected to shoot a deer. Then what is initially horrifying and frightening becomes tolerable, then even enjoyable, exciting, and addicting—this is the numbing process. In a similar way the appetite for violence in entertainment is created by the violent programming and then is constantly reinforced by the same programming. Sounds like an addiction, doesn't it?

As with many bad exposures, those least able to deal with them often get the biggest doses. Whether the environment involves urban exhausts and lead poisoning, advertisements for alcohol, liquor stores concentrated in poor communities, or exposure to violence, bad things happen with worse consequences to those already having a difficult time.

It is also startling to ponder the class and race issues involved in the entertainment media's reluctance to respond to the scientific evidence on the impact of violent programming and in the persistent portrayals of negative stereotypes of the poor and members of racial minorities. Poor children watch more television and are more likely to have parents who are not reading the latest magazines and books on parenting. If television itself isn't a source of information on the negative impact of violent programming on children, then these parents will be the last to know.

Bandura was one of the first to study the effects of media content on children.[12] As early as 1963, he concluded that exposure to violent or aggressive action in films not only increases the viewer's aggressive behavior but also determines the type of aggression the viewer may exhibit. The *aggressor effect*, sometimes called the *imitative effect* or *modeling response*, refers to this connection between viewing media violence and displaying aggressive or violent behavior. It is one of the main concerns among experts on the subject. Just as some children who are witnesses to real-world violence come to view aggression and violence as normal and even expected, some children exposed to large amounts of violent entertainment increasingly tend to view violence as a solution to their problems or conflicts.

Bandura's work has been followed by hundreds of subsequent studies repeatedly confirming this observation. Media violence is one of those windows in the slot machine. The overwhelming weight of the evidence from scientific studies is consistent and has been over the years: viewing or having a preference for violent television is related to aggressive attitudes, values, and behaviors. This result was true for the studies conducted when television was new and the measures of children's aggression were teachers' ratings. It is still true for the more recent studies (which number in the hundreds) with measures of aggressiveness that are substantially more sophisticated.

There is even strong evidence that very young children (infants and toddlers) imitate behavior they see on television. One study found that 65 percent of children as young as fourteen months were able to imitate the actions of an adult in an instructional video and manipulate a novel toy, whereas only 2 percent of those who didn't watch the video could do so.[13]

Girls Respond to Media Violence

Boys have generally been thought to be more adversely affected by television violence because violent behavior is usually exhibited by male characters. Many researchers have concluded that the differences in effects according to gender justify giving more attention to boys in their research. However, recent studies show that girls are also adversely affected, although in different ways. The 1986 study, mentioned earlier, that analyzed multiple previous studies suggests that the effect of aggressive role models and violence on television is significant for girls but must be measured differently because, historically, female characters on television are not as aggressive as male characters.[14] Even though girls who are heavy viewers of television violence may show a tendency toward aggressiveness, in that 1986 study they did not display aggressive behaviors or attitudes in the same way as boys. A 1991 study, mentioned earlier, also demonstrated gender differences in responses to television violence, with girls showing more subtle forms of antisocial behavior such as anxiety, irritability, and intolerance of delay.[15] These studies establish that there is an impact of television viewing on girls. We think that with television content changing and female images becoming more aggressive, the impact will also change, and girls will show responses similar to those of boys. In fact we think this is already happening; in a 2004 study, urban girls expressed attitudes that indicate they found thrill and enjoyment in fighting, a make-my-day attitude.[16] "Make my day" doesn't just mean be careful or you will get beaten up; it communicates a pleasure in fighting and a desire to take any little opportunity to beat you up.

Summing Up the Changes

So, what has changed? What explains the significant change in girls' behavior over the last few decades? What explains the increase in girls' arrest rates for violent crime at a time when boys' rates declined? It is obvious at this point that we believe it is the way this nation socializes girls that has changed. We believe that girls are now behaving more aggressively and violently because the entertainment media images now include the feminine superhero and because traumatized and victimized girls are externalizing their pain violently. It won't be long before girls will engage in more violent behavior for fun or status or power—much the way boys do.

We don't take these changes in behavior lightly. Changing the social norms and values that are spurring this behavior is essential. Yet often we feel like out-of-touch naysayers. While movies that are awe inspiring in their creativity and special effects glamorize violence and promote violent solutions to problems, we are writing books about how bad this is. It would be easier to ignore the changes, to pretend that girls are just not like that and that they will never have the same level of problems as boys do. Well, we can't. People thought similarly about crack, that girls and women would never neglect their children for crack. They did and they do. We saw (and still see) denial of the suburban and rural experiences with violence: "that would never happen in my community." And we see the numbers of girls being arrested. We can't ignore what we see. So one more time we are writing a book to say—let's all change now.

Part Two

Taking On the Challenge

Chapter Six

Tips for Parents

We estimate that parents tell their children to brush their teeth somewhere between 5,000 and 10,000 times during childhood. How often do you think parents tell children to develop nonviolent problem-solving skills? Or to recognize and manage their anger without fighting? Or even not to fight?

Just saying, "don't hit," to a child is like saying, "don't get cavities," without saying, "brush your teeth." You can't tell children just what not to do. Parents have to tell them what to do also. Actually, telling your child what should be done is only the first step. Parents have to teach them to do it, show them how to do it, and model the behavior as well. What to do when angry, how to problem solve, how to show respect and negotiate—these are just some of the skills that must be demonstrated. It is not enough to say, "don't fight." The alternatives to fighting must be taught.

The ART of Parenting

In this chapter, we introduce the ART of parenting model for parents to use to help children grow into healthy, assertive, and nonviolent adults who are capable of creative conflict resolution. The ART of parenting model has three parts:

A: Act as a role model—do rather than tell; demonstrate rather than dictate.

R: Reach out to others—build a community of caring adults around your child.

T: Talk and listen—communicate, communicate, and then communicate some more.

A: Act as a Role Model

The following story illustrates how much more important actions are than words. We were at a conference, and the speaker asked all of us in the audience to raise our hands and make an OK sign (holding a hand up in the air and forming an "O" with the thumb and index finger). He then asked everyone to put a hand on his or her chin. Even though he repeatedly said "chin," he simultaneously demonstrated what he wanted by putting his hand on his cheek. He continued to repeat "chin" but kept his hand on his cheek. Needless to say, most members of the audience had their hands on their cheeks. Saying one thing and doing another sends a mixed message, and this story illustrates a truism: it's what you do that has the greatest impact, not what you say.

Saying the right things to your daughter is important; she will hear, understand, and reflect back on things like, "try to talk through and negotiate a conflict"; "it's worth trying to put yourself in the other person's shoes when you are in a conflict with them"; "when angry, try counting to ten before you react." However, what you do is even more important for her. This is true for both mothers and fathers. Considerable research describes the important role of fathers in the lives of sons; much less attention has been given to fathers' importance to daughters. Both parents must model the behavior they want to see in their children because children imitate. Imitation is natural and essential; it is the way children learn what they need to know to survive.

As a pediatrician, Howard demonstrates to parents that even the youngest of infants imitates the behavior of adults. At the first visit, the two-week well-baby visit, he puts his face close to the infant's face and sticks out his tongue, purses his lips, and makes exaggerated movements with his mouth. What do you think the infant does? The infant begins to do the same things. You can teach a two-week-old infant to stick out her tongue!

Imitation is a lifesaving strategy used by young children (and adults for that matter) to learn and survive. Obviously, adults can see a behavior and not turn around and imitate it. Using the filters of experience, adults judge a behavior and make a decision whether to imitate it or not. Children don't have these filters of experience (they acquire them during the growing-up process). They will pretty much imitate everything they see. Whether you have thought about it or not, you are teaching your children at every turn.

Young Children Imitate Adults on Television. An unsettling and surprising series of studies from the 1980s demonstrate the capacity of fifteen- to eighteen-month-old toddlers to imitate the actions of an adult—an adult on television![1] Almost all the children in this toddler group were able to manipulate and open a toy and to play with the toy correctly after seeing a video of a man playing with the toy. In the toddler group that did not see the video, only a couple of the children were able to open and play with the toy. We knew that young children imitate the behaviors of adults and other children around them, but to find out that toddlers imitate and learn from adults on television was an eye-opener, even for us.

You may have heard of the famous Bobo the Clown beanbag study.[2] In this study of young children, the children continuously punched a beanbag after they saw a man on television punching a pop-up beanbag. Prior to watching the television, these children played with the bag very differently and no one punched it.

In many instances studies confirm what is already common knowledge, and that is the case here. We really don't have to tell you how closely your children watch what you do. They watch you, and they watch other adults (especially those on television) very closely, and they imitate what they see. It is difficult to be on stage 24/7, but you are when you become a parent. Here's the rule: if you want your child to do something, then you do it in front of her!

Being a Good Example Requires Improving Your Own Skills. Parents cannot teach what they don't know and don't practice themselves, a point we will come back to. You are your child's major example for ways to handle anger, conflict, hurt, and pain.

Every day you teach your children how to treat others, how to treat others who are different, and how to express feelings. The better you are at these skills, the better your children will be. We call these behaviors *skills* because they are just that. Skills must be taught and practiced. If your child wanted to be an Olympic gymnast, you wouldn't give her her first lesson at age fourteen. You wouldn't start her lessons at age five and then stop them at age fourteen. You wouldn't have her practice every once in a while. You would have her start early and practice regularly until she is ready. You would also hire a coach, someone who knows what she needs to know, to teach her and practice with her.

Acquiring conflict resolution skills is just like acquiring the skills for any sport. If children are to have Olympic gold medal–level conflict resolution skills, then they must be taught them early and they must practice often. You are your child's number one teacher and coach for life skills. However, life has many lessons to learn, so all of the adults around your daughter are also her life coaches to teach and model the behaviors she should learn.

Once we are adults it is not easy to admit that we need to learn better skills for getting along. We need to know how to tell people we are upset with them in an assertive manner that leads to a negotiation rather than an explosion and how to respond to people who are upset with us in a way that deescalates the situation and leads to a negotiation rather than a ruptured relationship or a fight. By adulthood most of us have figured out how to stay out of physical fights with other adults (there are not as many fights between adult coworkers as there are between children on a playground). However, most adults are pedestrian in their conflict resolution skills. Most take it, and take it, and take it some more, and then explode. The explosion seems justified because of all the time spent "taking it." Alternatively, situations are avoided and ignored—until the explosion of temper. Broken friendships, ruptured families, tense work settings, and even some litigation could be avoided with better conflict resolution skills.

Skills like giving "I" messages ("I feel bad when you speak to me that way") instead of "you" messages ("You are bad for talking to me like that") can go a long way toward setting the stage for a negotiation and acceptable resolution of a conflict. Learning to say something like, "What do you want me to do?" in a calm and sincere voice can help someone who is angry with you articulate the potential solution to a conflict and go a long way toward setting a negotiation table. Learning and practicing these skills will make you a better parent and will help you in the rest of your life as well.

We know adults can get better at their conflict resolution skills because, inadvertently, both of us have improved our skills over the last two decades. We describe this improvement as inadvertent because we didn't start this work to get better at conflict resolution ourselves; we started this work to teach children to get better. Like most adults, we thought we were pretty good at the skills of getting along. The work that we have done in the name of children has also been of tremendous benefit to our personal and professional lives.

The "A" in the ART of parenting model requires you to improve your conflict resolution skills so that you can be a model for your children. We want you to be intentional about teaching and modeling the skills to them at a very young age and practicing with them every day, just as you do with teaching them to brush their teeth. A great time to discuss these skills is when you are reading a book or watching television with your children. Most stories have conflict and can lead to a discussion of who uses the best interpersonal skills, who is the best problem solver, and how would someone who is very good at conflict resolution handle the situation. These discussions of fictional and real-life situations are important. Remember to ask, "What else could be done?" or, "How could he have avoided this situation in the first place?" to spark your children's creative thinking about conflict resolution and prevention.

Often the plots of movies and books focus on a crisis that could have been prevented, particularly if those involved had better conflict resolution skills. This is worth pointing out to your children over and over again, just as many times as you tell them to brush their teeth. Many of the scenarios that play out with physical violence have a history. The better children are at understanding that history or escalation phase, the better they will be at preventing fights.

Like adults, children can be short of solutions. When presented with a conflict, aggressive children have two responses: do nothing or beat the other person up. Some may put "tell the teacher" on that list, but often not with any real conviction or sense that the teacher is going to be helpful. What often happens in a conflict is that a child will do nothing, do nothing, do nothing, and then explode and fight the other person (sound familiar?).

The "A" in the ART of parenting is about your example, your actions. The "R" is about reaching out to others to get help. Seeking the help of other role models and confidants and finding other supports for your children can make a huge difference in your parenting capacity. Grandparents, godparents, aunts, uncles, extended family, and your friends can all be enlisted in service to your children. Ask for their help, creative thinking, and action—you are not in this by yourself. If you try to do it all, not only will you likely fall short on some of the necessary resources you need, but you will also miss the opportunity to set the stage for the teen years when your daughter may prefer to talk to and confide in someone else. If the stage is set via a prior relationship with another adult, then it is likely that the selected confidant will be someone you know and trust.

R: Reach Out to Others

As her parent, you along with family, friends, and teachers can make a big difference in the socialization of your daughter. Together you can buffer and counter much of the entertainment media junk coming at girls. The entertainment media's images of sexy, violent, feminine superheroes can be successfully challenged by parents and an extended network of caring adults if they are in it for the long haul and intentional about their role as conflict resolution role models.

Not only are these media images fake and easily debunked, but there is nothing more powerful in the lives of teenagers than an adult who is in it for the long term, cares, and is committed to helping.

Research has emphasized the importance of close, caring adult relations in the healthy development of young women. If your daughter is demonstrating risky behavior, then you will be especially interested in knowing the things that can help: positive role models, improved and appropriate relationship skills, enhanced self-esteem, a healthy individual identity, and a positive future orientation. When you reach out to other adults to help in the raising of your daughter, make sure they understand their role in her life and the things that can help. For example, nothing enhances self-esteem like accomplishment, in any arena. If you have a friend who is a photographer and your daughter is interested in photography (even if it may be a passing interest), don't hesitate to ask your friend to spend time with your daughter. Depending on where you are on the worry scale, you may even consider paying your friend to hire your daughter for a few hours a week after school. Sometimes you have to create the opportunities for your daughter to learn and accomplish. The less money you have, the more creative you may need to be.

Don't Feel You Have to Do Everything. Sometimes because of our own need to be involved and helpful, we want to do or try to do everything. Not only is this nearly impossible, especially as your child becomes a teenager, but there is often a period during a child's development when she, or he, is more likely to listen to others than to you. For example, you may experience your daughter as being difficult and refusing to respond to questions or expectations. Others, however, will tell you that your daughter is delightful, helpful, and very engaged. This is something we have both experienced. Children, and especially teenagers, often behave differently when their parents aren't around, and this means that others have opportunities to address issues that you find it impossible to get to. You can use this to your advantage by incorporating these persons into your repertoire of child-rearing strategies. Rather than fighting (or being jealous of) your child's interest in other people, reach out to them. Very intentionally involve them in the life of your child. Obviously (but we must say it here), we are not talking about anyone who may be a threat (sexually or physically). These must be people you trust, and you must monitor the relationships.

What If She's Not Really Talking to You? Often children are unable to talk to parents about an issue and will find it easier to confide in a trusted adult or extended family member. If this occurs (and it certainly happened to both of us with our daughters—though more with Deborah and Mimi than with Howard and Zoë), it will likely be during their teenage years. You will do better if you anticipate this period and put the trusted adults in place well before the teen years.

Here's the deal. Ask your best friends or relatives (godparents, aunts, and uncles, and so on) to have regular talks with your child. Ask them to take your child on an excursion once a month or so, starting at an early age. This sets the stage for future conversations that might be about more difficult subjects. If they have to establish the relationship and have the regular conversations in the absence of previous regular contact, it will be more difficult. But obviously, even in the latter case, having another person with whom your daughter can discuss difficult issues can be a literal lifesaver.

A Professional Caregiver Can Come in Handy. A pediatrician who has taken care of your child since her early years can be a great source of help to parents of teen daughters. If (for whatever reason) your daughter does not have that kind of relationship with her doctor, find a professional caregiver and help a relationship develop. You can identify someone, set up the appointment, go with your daughter to the first appointment, and make sure to set the right stage by describing (with both your daughter and the caregiver present) the confidential relationship you expect them to have. It is important for your daughter to know that you do not expect the doctor, nurse, social worker, school counselor, or other caregiver to reveal the content of the conversations she has with your daughter, unless it is life threatening. Actually, you can let the professional describe the circumstances under which she would break a confidence. In this situation it is critical for your daughter to understand the nature of the relationship with a caregiver.

Deborah used this strategy during her daughter's "I'm not really liking you too much" period. Mimi's pediatrician served in this role. Deborah selected her during Mimi's older childhood years so that Mimi would have a woman physician to care for her during her later teen years. At twenty-three, Mimi still visits that pediatrician on occasion, even though her care is now in adult settings.

This trusted professional does not have to be a physician. The important piece of this approach is that she has a good relationship with your daughter (or seems capable of establishing one) and understands the role you want her to play in your daughter's life. Also, it is critical that you let your daughter know that you will not talk behind her back or separately to the caregiver. If you have something that concerns you, you will speak about it with both your daughter and the professional present. If you absolutely must discuss it without your daughter present, *do not discuss it while your daughter sits in the waiting room*. If the caregiver asks to speak with you without your daughter, do so. Ideally, she will have told your daughter that she is going to speak with you and what she will discuss. If she has not, ask her to do so. Remember, this professional relationship is for your daughter, not for you. Get your own relationship with a provider if you are feeling left out or if you want to talk.

Get to Know the Parents of Friends.   Part of building a community around your daughter is getting to know her friend's parents. This allows for discussions with other parents about adult supervision in such areas as setting boundaries and curfews and knowing what the rules and expectations are at different houses. This network of parents can create uniform boundaries and ensure safety and consistency in terms of expectations and rules, develop better strategies for problem solving, aim for consistency in modeling behavior, and establish a support system for all of the involved parents so they can get help and have a place to vent (which parents of teenage girls certainly need). It also gives a clear message to your daughter and all the other daughters of the group, a message that you and all the other parents are invested in and care about her. Furthermore it creates a social environment that promotes truthfulness for everyone involved.

T: Talk and Listen

The "T" in the ART of parenting means talk and listen. Communication is key, and listening is even more important than talking. No matter what your daughter does, do not cut the lines of communication. You are the adult, and you must get over any hurt feelings, anger, embarrassment, or guilt you may feel and keep the lines of communication open—even in (especially in) a crisis.

Talking and Listening Tactics. Even if the two of you are going through a "phase" in which your daughter is not talking to you very much, don't stop talking and listening to her. Listening is really the key. You must practice listening without overreacting. You must practice the kind of listening that allows your daughter to vent. Sometimes the most verbally aggressive daughters, during their worst phases, seem to spew venom from their mouths. Don't let this throw you. Let them know that venom spewing is inappropriate, but don't stop talking to them and don't start spewing venom back (that's the hard part). Staying cool and not spewing venom back is truly hard. Even harder is not taking it as a personal assault. Not every daughter goes through this phase, but those that do are really difficult to have around. Remember that it is just a phase and that you are the adult. As the adult, you can be calm and get over it.

You can definitely say things like, "Why don't you go to your room and come back when you are calm," or, "I can't take it when you are screaming such horrible things; you let me know when you can talk about this without trying to hurt my feelings," or, "I am really trying to understand, but I won't be able to if you keep attacking me and I won't stay here while you verbally attack me like that." You can make it clear that her words are hurtful and inappropriate. You can require that she calm down before you engage in conversations. All of that is appropriate, but don't stop talking to her because your feelings are hurt. You can request an apology from her if you think she was out of line—but don't stop talking or listening to her.

In the Car—A Great Time to Talk.   Difficult conversations are sometimes best had in the car. Howard's wife introduced him to this strategy, and it works. We have both tried it with great success and have since heard others who have tried this strategy for good and effective conversations with their children. In the car you don't have to make eye contact. In the car you have a defined period of time—usually short—to talk. In the car you are both captive with few distractions. In the car is a great time for conversation. You should ask questions and not push. Listen more than you talk; often the less you ask, the more you get.

Don't expect to get all of the information at one time; be willing to let some things drop for the moment. Don't tell your daughter what to do (unless she asks you), but be willing to tell her what you will do. For example, if she tells you she is going to do something you do not want her to do, rather than tell her no, tell her what you will do in response. Ultimately, you cannot make her do something or not do something, but you can make it clear what the consequences are going to be as a result of her behavior. As your daughter gets older, you have less control over her, but you certainly can and should share with her what you will do.

Sticking with ART

The ART model contains basic, easy-to-remember concepts. Unfortunately, it is sometimes difficult to adhere to them. Keep the concepts in mind and practice them. You will definitely get better at them over time. That is the good news. You don't have to be perfect to be a good parent, and you can learn what you need to know. Some parents who had exceptional parents themselves have a concrete example they can follow. It is a bit easier for them, because they have learned through their own rearing what is expected and some of what works. But even in those situations, especially because a lot has changed in this society, parents can find themselves flying by the seat of their pants when it comes to what to do.

Parenting, a nearly universal, extremely important, and very difficult responsibility, is not a required subject in school. Therefore those who didn't have great examples in their own parents have an even harder task ahead. But regardless of how good or bad a job your parents did, you can be a great parent. The ART model is just one approach—one that we think can help parents prevent all types of problems that can occur in the adolescent years. Following the ART model can also help parents respond to problems when they do occur. But what about violence? How do you help your daughter prevent and deal with violence?

Violence and Your Daughter

It is very important to discuss violence directly with your daughter because she may encounter situations where it occurs or is likely. Most of the recent writings about girls and aggression are filled with discussions of the "alternative" ways that girls fight, particularly middle-class, suburban white girls. Although that is an accurate description of girls' fighting in the recent past, we don't assume that it will stay that way. Society has learned that the violence didn't stay among poor urban boys and young men and should be learning that violence has not remained a problem just for boys. We are assuming that physical violence will not remain a problem just for poor urban girls. The way it starts with violence is not the way it remains; this is one of the most important lessons for parents.

Parents had to learn that telling boys to go back outside and fight something out is poor advice when there is a chance someone has a knife or a gun at the end of the street. Now, parents have to learn that girls are capable of physical violence and may begin to demonstrate more violent behaviors toward other girls, particularly with such new images on the nation's movie screens as the beautiful, angelic blond who will slice off your head in a cold minute (aka Uma Thurman's character in *Kill Bill*). The backbiting and bullying behavior that parents of girls were able to ignore in the past as less important or just temporarily painful may now become the source of serious violent crimes, just as it has for boys.

Before a "girl Columbine" occurs, let's act on the preponderance of evidence that girls and boys are not that different in their capacity for violence, that violence is learned, and that society sets the parameters for how children will behave. Let's not forget the role of the media in setting those parameters. And most important, let's act because of the changing statistics.

Whether they are girls or boys, hurt children find a way to express their pain, often in destructive ways. Traditionally, girls would internalize the pain and use self-destructive measures. More recently, they seem to have perfected the use of sneaky, below the radar, and underhanded externalization (girl bullying). Boys have traditionally externalized more, with physical aggression and violent outbursts near the top of their repertoire.

Things have changed, are changing, and may continue to change along the behavioral spectrum, with girls coming to more closely resemble boys. Many have assumed that what happened in other neighborhoods in the first wave of youth violence wouldn't happen in theirs. They assumed that girls were "nice" and boys weren't—until the recent rash of writings about mean girls. Let's not fall into the trap of assuming that only boys or "deviant" girls will use physical violence—so that we have to learn differently the hard way. The current statistics should be enough, enough to convince all of us of the possibility of serious girl violence—yes, even in the suburbs.

Some Violence Prevention Parenting Tips

How can parents go about preventing girls' violence? In the rest of the chapter we discuss preventing dating violence and intervening when bullying occurs. We also answer some questions parents often ask us. First, consider these general violence prevention tips.

1. Teach girls to be nonviolent and nonvictim.
2. Teach and model healthy assertiveness.
3. Don't trivialize the pain felt by bullied children.
4. Don't overlook adult bullies and institutional bullies (racism and sexism).
5. Remember that the adults at school may not respond to threats made by a child against another child or may not know how to respond.
6. Be willing to help change your child's environment— make new friends, change your place of worship, and so on.
7. Celebrate your child's accomplishments.
8. Use creative punishment that promotes healthy activities and sets the stage for more accomplishments to celebrate (as discussed later in this chapter).
9. Use role playing—even at home and even among siblings.
10. Introduce your child to new friends.
11. Ask your adult friends to help you with your child.
12. Get a professional caregiver involved in your child's life early on.
13. If your child's behavior hurts you, let her know it, but remember that you are the adult—don't stop talking or listening to your child.
14. Don't excuse your child's bad behavior, but don't overreact either. Punish or discipline in ways that help your daughter develop the skills and capacity to be a healthy adult.
15. Get to know the parents of your daughter's friends; create a network.

Dating Violence and Your Daughter

Girls are victimized more than they fight or victimize others. Although that may be changing, it is crucial to understand that protecting your daughter from dating violence situations is also your responsibility. There are several resources to help you understand dating violence and strategies for preventing it (see the listings on dating violence in the Resources section of this volume). A very good strategy for helping your daughter avoid negative situations with boyfriends is to ensure that she understands the difference between a boyfriend who is good and one who isn't.

Good Boyfriend	Bad Boyfriend
Cares what you do	Wants to control what you do
Expresses himself without putting you down	Puts you down verbally
Can disagree with you pleasantly	Considers a disagreement a threat
Validates your feelings	Questions your feelings
Builds your confidence	Causes you to doubt yourself
Encourages you	Makes you feel discouraged
Can enjoy your friends	Says bad things about your friends
Does not hit or threaten when angry	Hits or makes you afraid

No boyfriend will be perfect, and one problem should not destroy a relationship. However, teach your daughter that if a boyfriend ever hits her, she should leave that relationship alone. The warning signs just listed are important because physical violence often comes after her judgment has been terribly warped by his control over her, including isolating her from other opinions. The earlier in a relationship that she is able to recognize the signs of abuse and control and break off, the better. Knowing the difference between concern and control is not always easy, but it is crucial to know. The difference between "I don't really like that dress" and "I am not going to go with you if you wear that" is significant. The difference between "I don't understand why you feel that way" and "You shouldn't feel that way" is significant. Your job description includes helping your daughter learn what makes a good friend or boyfriend and what doesn't.

Teach your daughter to avoid people who fight because they are not safe to be around. As a general rule, anyone who hits anyone to express himself or herself is not good to be around. Children who fight may be popular, but they are not safe.

Talk to your daughter about boyfriends and how to select them. Make it clear to her that a boy who hits anyone or anything is a concern (this is also true of a girl who hits of course). His violence may not be directed at her at the outset, but any violence toward anyone is concerning. It is a signal that he could become violent toward her or endanger her by behaving violently toward others. Again, anyone who hits anyone to express anger is just not safe to be around.

Dealing with a Bully: How Much Do You Intercede?

Bullying is learned behavior (a child learns to feel good at the expense of someone else) that is in part precipitated by another's appearance of vulnerability (different clothing, skin color, accent, or anything else for that matter). Much of the work on girls' aggression suggests that your daughter too may experience bullying, especially in the form of gossip, character assassination, or exclusion. Your daughter may also be a bystander to bullying or may be the bully herself.

Like other parenting strategies, the ART of parenting model is a general approach that can be applied to almost every issue or problem related to behavior. Here are some ideas for applying it to bullying.

A: *Act as an Example.* It is important to be an example of appropriate ways of interacting with others. Showing children how to negotiate and get what they want and need without intimidating or bullying is important. You can help your daughter avoid bullying by role modeling appropriate ways of interacting with others, especially around negotiation and getting what you want. If she sees that being pushy, physically or verbally, works for those around her, she is likely to imitate that behavior with friends and schoolmates. If parents use intimidation to work out conflict with each other or with their children, they are essentially teaching their children that strategy. Teaching respect for others and demonstrating nonintimidating interpersonal skills through your own actions teaches children that they can get what they want in more prosocial ways.

Using putdowns in interactions with others—friends, family members, and your children—teaches them that this is an acceptable way to talk to others. Using more constructive ways of communicating teaches an alternative way of relating. Demonstrating ways of expressing anger that are not hurtful to others shows your daughter that she does not have to hurt others to make herself feel better.

Make a conscious effort to respond to situations in a way that models the way you want your daughter to behave and to treat others. This requires constant thought and self-reflection and practice. In your role as parent, you are your daughter's teacher and her constant reminder that excellent interpersonal skills will come in handy throughout her life, in both personal and professional situations.

Express your feelings when you are treated badly, called names, or intimidated during an interaction. This helps your daughter understand the impact of bullying behaviors and models one strategy for dealing with it. When you express how painful it is to be ignored or disrespected, you demonstrate that *using words* is one way to deal with things you do not like. Bullies, because they are looking for group approval, often retreat when verbally confronted with their attempt to hurt others.

If your daughter calls you a name or speaks to you disrespectfully, make sure to tell her how you feel (using those "I" messages), and if necessary to deescalate the situation, remain silent or walk away. Say something like, "I feel terrible. Why do you want to hurt my feelings?" and, "I will talk with you later when we both are calm." Do not stop speaking to her over a long period of time. She may owe you an apology but don't let that cause you to stop speaking to her for an extended period. You will get your apology, but maybe not until she is twenty. In the meantime, remember you are the adult, and she needs you to talk to her. Staying silent is a choice when the only other option is exploding in anger. Responding to her with anger will escalate the situation and make it harder to communicate in the future.

Teenagers, irrespective of how they may act, want your approval and your attention. As with younger children, how you react to their behavior teaches them what works and doesn't work and models responses that they can use if they are treated similarly.

R: Reach Out to Others. Reaching out to others creates opportunities to get more information about the things that are going on in your daughter's peer group. You might find out that bullying is going on from others before you hear it from your daughter. Don't be shy about checking in with other parents from time to time. Ask how things are going and whether they witnessed any behaviors of concern the last time they were caring for the group. Within the network of parents, share information in a way that allows you to understand the peer group's dynamics and prevent or respond effectively to any bullying.

A network of parents in communication with each other allows more consistent parental responses to any issue, especially bullying if it is playing out in the peer group. Your child may not tell you directly if members of the group are having issues with other kids at school or in the neighborhood, especially if she is involved. It is often easier to address a group bullying process when you are working in concert with others.

T: Talk and Listen.   Talking with and listening to your daughter is crucial to finding out if things are not going well. It creates an opportunity for you to share how you feel about behaviors such as bullying and affords an opportunity to discuss with your daughter how to deal with difficult situations. Key in this effort is holding off on your own thoughts about such things and first asking her what she thinks about the situation—Why is it happening? What can be done about it? Who might help? That sends a clear message that you are interested in her thoughts and are not going to jump to conclusions or judgments without hearing what she has to say.

Ask about bullying from time to time. Almost one-third of kids are directly involved in bullying (as the bully or the bullied), and all play the role of observers. It is therefore likely that your daughter is being affected by this in one way or another, and it is a subject of great relevance to most kids. If your child is being bullied, don't minimize the impact of hurt feelings.

Should You Tell the Teacher?

This is a difficult question. There are obvious situations that mandate that you go the school and speak up and obvious ones that you should let your daughter handle—and a lot of gray in between. Remember your ultimate goal as a parent—helping your child become a happy, healthy, and competent adult. Also make sure you find out what your daughter thinks about your going to the school and get her recommendations about the people with whom you should and shouldn't speak. Do not put yourself in the middle of something without your daughter's consent unless the situation is life threatening. If you think your daughter is in some danger, *go to the school* (and everywhere else for that matter) *and ask for help*.

If it is a usual conflict, decide with your daughter what should be done. She is in school every day, and if something is done that embarrasses her at school, she could be even further humiliated.

Frequently Asked Questions
and Creative Punishments

Parents often ask us what to do about certain situations. Here are our suggestions, some of which involve what we call *creative punishments*, punishments designed to help children try new approaches.

1. How can I tell if my daughter is moving in a dangerous direction?

There are several ways you can tell if your daughter is getting involved in violence. One of the most important signs is a change in normal patterns of behaviors, moods, or friendships. Not wanting to go to school, avoiding certain friends, and changes in schoolwork or performance are examples of this change. Even when not related specifically to violence, these are common signs that something is wrong, and making an effort to observe them is key to picking up on problems early. Often, subtle changes are warning signs that if heeded can help you deal with a problem before it has gone too far.

Here, the "T" in ART is particularly useful. Talking regularly with your daughter is the most effective way of seeing behaviors or situations of concern in their early stages. Being asked about bullying, fighting, and other signs of risky situations is often a relief to kids who are stressed and are searching for a way to tell someone. A simple no or shrug may be all you get at first, and it is best not to push, but these questions tell your daughter that you are interested in these issues and may result in her bringing it up later or on future queries from you. If you don't ask such questions or bring up these subjects, then your daughter can't tell what interests you or might be a subject she can raise with you.

2. What do I do if I feel that I have lost control over my daughter?

This is where the "R" in the ART model becomes extremely important. If you have lost control, then it is important to get help from others. Reach out to your minister, school guidance counselor, daughter's physician, or the parent of your daughter's friend—whoever you think can be helpful. If your daughter seems to have a good relationship with one of her teachers, start with that. Depending on the circumstances you may have to reach out to the most responsible of your daughter's friends and get his or her help. Get advice from one of these people, and find out how to help your daughter succeed at something—art, track, French, typing, something! Nothing helps a turnaround like some small successes.

If your daughter is in some kind of danger, you may need to reach out to the school or local police for their advice. We have heard the stories of parents or grandparents in desperate situations who worked with the police to have their child arrested in order to begin a turnaround. Another drastic measure we have heard of is moving to another city to get children away from dangerous influences who have gotten too close. We are not recommending a drastic measure—you have to be the judge of that—but we are recommending that you get the advice and help of others, particularly professionals who can influence your daughter.

If she is already in trouble then there are likely to be helping professionals already involved. Work with them to come up with a game plan to move forward. Don't forget to build on your daughter's strengths while working on the problems. We can't say it enough. Nothing turns a situation around better than a series of small successes. Find something to applaud along the way. When parents say things like, "at least she is coming home at night," or, "it could be worse," they are applauding the things that they can along the way and keeping themselves from feeling overwhelmed. Face the facts and find the positive (even if it is just a kernel).

Using the ART model in the situation where you feel a loss of control means reaching out to others so that they can do some of the role modeling and the talking and listening for you.

3. What do I do if my younger daughter is following in her sister's bad footsteps?

We are sure this is a scary situation for you when you have one daughter who has run away, is in jail, or is drug addicted and a second one seems to be going wrong as well. ART applies here as well, and again, the reach out to others becomes your central strategy (see the answer to the previous question about loss of control). In this situation use prevention efforts like making sure your daughter is involved in healthy after-school activities that consume most of her time and allow her some success. An added benefit of these extracurricular activities is that they provide some additional caring, competent adults for you to use as allies in the effort to carve a safe and healthy path for your daughter (and these adults can really come in handy if things go wrong).

You will need to be as creative as possible in helping your daughter select the after-school activities that are best for her. Often parents feel they should take away activities as a punishment for breaking the rules. We argue against this to a certain extent. Taking away privileges like going to a party or going out with friends to a movie is not a problem; however, taking away track, or yearbook club, or cheerleading for that matter could be a problem. Not only does this punishment take away the opportunities for healthy involvement with other teens and adults, it diminishes your child's opportunities to have other caring adults in her life, and more important, it diminishes her opportunities for success at something. Classroom work is not going to be every child's strong suit, and some will find their talents uncovered in other areas.

4. What if grounding her isn't working?

Grounding, taking away a cell phone, and taking away car privileges are the mainstays of punishing teenagers. These strategies have a place and should be used where appropriate and effective. If overused, used for an extended period, or if used for minor offenses, they can become less effective and difficult to enforce. Deborah started using involvement in after-school activities as punishment. At the age when her daughter was "too cute" and "too grown" and "too important" to be involved with anyone except her friends (you know that thirteen to fifteen age range), Deborah and her husband decided once when they needed to punish her that she would have to select and join two after-school activities of which one had to be a sport. She joined track, which became her high school sport, and Mimi (who is now a twenty-three-year-old, working college graduate) still holds an unbroken high school track record in Massachusetts.

These creative punishment methods continued and included taking her on business trips over the weekend (for example, to a church-sponsored conference on violence in the community) and taking her to see movies of Deborah's choice. (*Glory* and *Killing Fields*, which show violence but are based on true stories and capture the pain, tragedy, and senselessness of violence, were two of the choices.) Going places with Deborah was not on her daughter's top ten list of things to do, so these punishments also served the dual purpose of giving the two of them time together that they wouldn't otherwise have had and exposing Mimi to things and ideas different from those expressed by her friends.

Creative punishment takes both children and parents out of their usual roles and is a direct effort to have punishment help children become healthy and happy adults. The key principles are

1. That you require your daughter to participate in something healthy and positive that she wouldn't do on her own (go to a conference with you, to a musical, the opening of the symphony, and so on). The activity should be something that has a school field trip quality to it.

2. That at least one parent has to participate as well (unless you require that your daughter choose an after-school activity or other activity that is organized and supervised by some other adult).

3. That you avoid "scared straight" kinds of activities. Not only will you both have trouble enjoying these see-what-bad-consequences-there-are activities but the literature suggests

that these kinds of experiences are not helpful and can actually glamorize bad behavior and bad outcomes. This is an opportunity for you to show positive outcomes and inspire your daughter into good behavior.

It's okay and actually great if you and your daughter wind up enjoying yourselves (so choose something interesting, and don't forget that because you are punishing her, you—not your daughter—get to choose what it is you do together!). If you have noticed that she has an interest in fashion, you might chose a lecture by a fashion magazine editor. Use your local newspaper's calendar section to expand the possibilities and choices. Be creative! You might require that she go with you to a monthly activity for three months or that she and you spend thirty minutes every night reading to each other. Remember the goal—a healthy, happy adult. Another benefit of creative punishments is that they are easier to enforce than the usual ones of grounding and taking away the cell phone. Parenting is hard, but a little creativity can go a long way toward easing some of the burden.

Practicing the ART Model

No matter how old your daughter is, you can put the ART model into practice. Act as a role model for your child. Reach out to others to help you and to set the stage for the teen years. Talk and listen and never cut the lines of communication, no matter how difficult or hurtful it gets for you. Use the in-the-car strategy—it works!

Add violence to the list of concerns facing you and your daughter. Be as intentional about addressing those issues as you are (or once were) about helping her brush her teeth. Show her what to do, show her how to do it, and make sure she practices. The ART model can help you raise a nonviolent, assertive young woman who is skilled at managing anger, resolving conflict, and solving problems.

Chapter Seven

Tips for Teachers and Schools

Allison had everything going for her. She was the second of three children in an upper-middle-class family, a sophomore in her local public high school, and doing great. Allison was socially popular, an A-student, a junior varsity cheerleader, and a star on the junior varsity field hockey team. She was dating a varsity basketball player, had been invited to the senior prom, and had recently been invited to pledge in the most sought-after sorority at her school. Things were just about perfect!

She even got along with her parents, who were understanding of her moodiness and need for privacy but were around when she needed help or advice.

Then things changed dramatically. Her moodiness increased. Her schoolwork fell behind. She spent more time alone and even cancelled plans with friends and her boyfriend. Her parents became concerned and began to wonder if she were involved in drugs. Their questions and concerns were met with shrugs and dismissals and finally by comments that she was "just going through some adolescent things." Then one afternoon her mother came home to find her asleep. Unable to arouse her, her mother then discovered an empty bottle of Tylenol lying in the sink. Allison was rushed to the hospital and, very fortunately, was successfully treated.

Her parents could not understand how this came about so suddenly and without any identifiable cause. Her mother searched her room for drugs and instead found her diary under the mattress. There she found the answers to her questions.

For the last several weeks Allison had been writing descriptions of what appeared to be a tortuous and mean-spirited hazing process for the school sorority. She experienced physical and verbal assaults and abuse and was given demeaning tasks, about which she wrote that she felt singled out, as if her popularity and successes had made her a target for the most severe treatment. She received threats that if she told anyone what was going on she would suffer even more. Unreasonable demands were made of her. She was expected to do mean and physically aggressive things to other girls. Her mother was shocked, even more so by the fact that this sorority was school sanctioned. How could this have happened? How could the school have missed it? How could girls behave like this?

Needless to say, her parents and the school responded, and Allison recovered and returned to her former self or at least got reasonably close.

The school leaders were shocked that this had occurred on their watch. They had clear rules but spent most of their energy ensuring that the fraternities were monitored, not the sororities. They assumed the risk of such hazing behavior was a boy thing; certainly girls were not at risk. This was a painful way to learn that things were not so simple. And it was even more painful when they began to realize this behavior was not completely new. Other girls began to speak up about their own experiences, and the leaders of the hazing confessed that they were just doing what they had experienced themselves. It was the norm; the expected thing to do.

The Changing School Experience

Sadly, this is not an isolated incident. From teachers, principals, and students, we have heard of a number of such episodes and practices. Some of these have even come to light in the press, but these news stories reflect only the tip of the iceberg. These hazing behaviors are not limited to sororities and fraternities either. Hazing is fairly common in school clubs and athletic teams. In fact, 79 percent of the NCAA athlete respondents to a survey reported experiencing one or more typical hazing behaviors (humiliation, degradation, abuse, or endangerment).[1] For this study initiation activities were defined as *acceptable* (preseason training, keeping a certain grade-point average, doing volunteer service, and the like), *questionable* (being yelled at, cursed at, or forced to wear embarrassing clothing; acting as a personal servant), and *unacceptable* (sexual harassment, confinement, being paddled or abandoned). The study found that 96 percent of the boys and 97 percent of the girls reported acceptable initiation activities, 68 percent of the boys and 63 percent of the girls reported questionable initiation activities, and *27 percent of the boys and 21 percent of the girls reported unacceptable initiation activities*. In addition, 52 percent of the boys and 51 percent of the girls reported "alcohol-related" initiation activities, which was startling because many of them were under the legal drinking age of twenty-one. Nor is hazing just a college problem. In another study, 48 percent of high school students who were a part of any group at school reported being subjected to some form of hazing. In his recent book *High School Hazing: When Rites Become Wrongs*, Hank Nuwer details the numbers and also discusses the frightening vulnerability of high school–aged adolescents that is embedded in their need to belong to a group.[2]

There are gender differences in hazing, with boys being more likely to report beatings and being required to steal or to vandalize property. They also report being tied up and confined to small places. Girls report less physical violence than boys, though a surprisingly large number of girls who are athletes report being hit or beaten. Girls are more likely to report receiving psychological and emotional putdowns and being required to perform demeaning antics in public.

Recently, schools are reporting hazing practices, increasing episodes of fighting among girls (sometimes with serious physical injury), mean-spirited interactions among girls and from girls toward teachers, and more. The standard responses consist of disbelief, uncertainty about what to do, and if anything, an expansion of *zero tolerance* (or *no tolerance*) policies that are primarily predicated on the threat of severe punishment—expulsion in particular—as the primary deterrent to fighting. But these policies are not working well, in the same way that they have not worked well with boys or at the community level in efforts to reduce youth violence.

Schools: Too Important to Overlook

It is by no means surprising that schools have been the leading source of the stories we have heard about the changing behavior of girls with respect to violence. Kids spend more time at school than anyplace else other than home. It isn't that schools are dangerous places but they are often the places where new trends are observed because of the amount of time youths spend there. It isn't that the school environment is toxic, or any more toxic than other places in the community, but that doesn't mean schools cannot be settings for violence among girls. It is also clear from the experiences at schools that much of girls' violence is girl on girl and not the more historically traditional form in which girls are victims of boys' violence. Some of the violence is also girls on boys; this remains relatively rare but not absent by any means. The problem for schools is that much of their effort in violence prevention has been focused on boys. The attention given to girls has focused primarily on their risks of victimization and to a lesser extent on their roles as bystanders or instigators of conflicts and fights.

However, there is much that schools can do. And there is much that parents can do to help, advocate, push, or initiate in collaboration with teachers and school personnel. Replicating strategies used for boys is not the answer, as girls have different needs, role models, pressures, and views of the world. Parents, teachers, and others can learn from their experiences with boys but must always place these lessons into the context of the social and cognitive world of girls.

Setting the Stage: The ART Model

The climate and environment of a school is central to any violence prevention effort. The physical environment; the role models; the nonverbal messages in posters, art, or signs; and the rules and expectations are all part of the school climate. The ART model for parenting, described in the previous chapter, applies here with some modifications. It provides a structure in most settings for thinking about strategies and planning programs for prevention work with children.

A: Act as a Role Model

The strategy of acting as a role model should be used by teachers, who are in a parental role at school, and also by all other school personnel, from senior administrators to maintenance staff to monitors in informal, nonclassroom settings. Kids learn from the behaviors they see around them outside the home as they do at home. Given that a majority of teachers are women, schools present an important opportunity for modeling prosocial behavior to girls. Addressing violence with girls is somewhat more complicated than it is with boys because of the balance that must be struck between being nonviolent and being nonvictim. School personnel are in a strong position to demonstrate nonviolent problem solving and illustrate nonvictim values as well.

But role modeling is only a part of the "A" component of the ART model in the school setting. Providing curricula and learning opportunities that influence values and behaviors is an important companion to this modeling. Skills for conflict resolution and dealing with anger are crucial, and although the fundamental approaches for girls are similar to those for boys (using "I" messages instead of "you" messages, for example), the context for girls is often very different. For example, a brewing conflict for a boy might start with an overt, non-game-related tackle on the football field—a

situation he may be able to defuse with a direct apology or by saying "excuse me." A girl may be drawn into a situation by the gos-
siping and behind-the-back talking of others. This more covert
conflict can escalate because there is much less opportunity to nip
it in the bud. In this situation a girl who has a sense that something
is brewing can chose to speak to one of the other girls involved in
an attempt to make friends with her or just defuse the conflict. "I"
messages would be helpful in both these situations, but the skills to
know what is wrong, when to address the conflict, and how and
whom to approach are different.

In order to generate authentic discussion and realistic strategies
for girls, schools must involve developmental experts in the process
of planning and teaching skills. Girls must be included as well. In
our work in one Boston high school with a girls' group, we asked
them to help us develop ways to prevent violence among girls. We
learned the importance of stress in the lives of the girls in the group
even though that was not what we were trying to understand. At
the insistence of the girls and despite our efforts to focus on violence prevention, we let them talk about the stress they experienced. We learned a lot, and the subsequent violence prevention
efforts at that school included the stress component. Including a
variety of girl students in the process can be extremely helpful.

In addition, learning opportunities in violence prevention must
be linked with such related issues as dating violence. This allows
teachers to help students learn the empowerment skills needed to
avoid or prevent victimization at the same time that nonviolent
problem solving is addressed. Separating these issues and the related
skill development may result in conflicting messages about behavior and values, which are likely to lead to confusion for many girls.

Another area to incorporate into violence prevention is media
literacy. This is essential to helping girls deal with the images of
beauty, desirability, and violent behavior that they see in movies,
on TV, in advertising, and on the Internet. Skills in decision making and behavior are best addressed in combination with the skills
needed to deal with the toxic messages that promote unhealthy and

risky behavior and values. Critical thinking is essential to helping girls deal with violence and is also a core skill in general in today's education system.

It is important to understand that the teaching of all these skills need not be separated from other basic core curricula at the school. For example, readings in English and literature courses can be used as a foundation for raising these topics and can provide a great opportunity for discussions about the subject. Health classes can and should address these issues as well, given that violence has a great impact on health behaviors and health itself. Nor do girls and boys need to be separated when addressing these subjects. Boys can certainly learn from girls; conflict resolution and nonviolent problem solving are areas in which girls may have better skills as they have historically been more socialized to use such skills. It is also helpful for girls to gain an understanding of how boys perceive these issues as well. There may be times when girls need opportunities to address these issues without boys present, but for the most part it is useful to have girls and boys together in the learning process.

R: Reach Out to Others

The reaching out and building a community component of violence prevention is also quite relevant in the school setting.

Respect and Tolerance as Basic Values. Practicing the basic values of the school community is an important learning experience for students. Having respect for others and viewing fighting or meanness as totally unacceptable are important elements of a healthy community. This, however, does not mean there is a need for punitive zero tolerance policies. Responding to disrespect, fighting, and meanness requires, first, teaching, practicing, and rewarding conflict resolution skills. Second, the signals that something deeper is going on need to be recognized and addressed. Expulsion leads to a missed opportunity to evaluate and remediate and also excludes the girls who may be most in need of support and inclusion. So the school community must have rules and expectations with clear consequences, but this approach must be linked to helpful responses, treatment, support, and understanding.

Incorporating understanding and empathy into the mix addresses another key component of skill development—tolerance. Teaching and modeling tolerance is another important element of a healthy school community. The kids who do bad or wrong things face consequences, but should also receive help, imparting values of tolerance and model discipline that is constructive, educational, and helpful. Most youths, girls included, learn far better from discipline that is strategic and educational than from punishment that imparts neither values nor learning nor recognition of the underlying factors that may be causing the negative behaviors. To punish without understanding the underlying factors or the opportunity to learn from the experience does not make things better and may in fact give the unintended message that whatever else is going on is neither relevant nor fixable.

To some, all this may sound as though we are just bleeding hearts who don't get it. We counter this with the fact that there is good science that shows that children and youths learn better from positive experiences than negative ones and that punitive discipline is far less effective in changing behavior than constructive discipline that teaches alternatives and rewards change. This is true for parents and true for schools.

Schools as Multiservice Centers. A second component of the reaching out and building a community strategy involves understanding that no one sector can do all of the necessary skills development alone. This means that schools and teachers need to reach out to others for assistance and collaboration in the same way that parents need to reach out to others in the process of raising healthy children.

Schools need others to help them develop effective violence prevention in general, and this is especially important for programs for girls as we all have so little experience with this. Many communities have professionals in health, public health, juvenile justice, mental health, and other fields who can be useful consultants and partners in this work. Many will help because they care about the health of girls and will not necessarily require payment for their involvement. Parents are also resources when considering options and approaches. And they are essential partners in the most successful approaches to preventing bullying. Turning to others not only broadens the base of people working on prevention strategies but also provides a constructive and positive opportunity for schools to engage parents in the life of the school for reasons other than that their child is having problems. Parents need opportunities to engage with schools that are not linked to an issue with their child, and schools are often searching for ways of bringing parents into the school setting for constructive activities. Violence prevention provides that opportunity, and many parents are excited to participate in activities that help their children build strong and healthy values. Teachers and parents want many of the same things, and a violence prevention effort is one concrete way for this desire to play this out.

Reaching out is essential to effectively helping kids in trouble—again especially girls, who are often left out of the picture when plans for remediation and help are developed. How often are girls with learning disabilities left unnoticed because boys are labeled as having a higher risk than girls for learning problems? How often are girls given promotions even when academically behind (so called social promotions) because they are viewed as less of a problem than boys? Isn't this one of the reasons that teachers and school administrators are at such a loss about what to do when they realize that girls are starting to fight "just like the boys" or even worse than the boys. This is a new problem (or at least newly recognized), and new collaborations are needed to address it.

Identifying ways to bring in other services for girls is essential. Mental health, physical health, youth development, outreach, and other services specifically focused on girls need to be either in-tegrated into school settings so that teachers are not left to fend on their own, or at the very least, relationships with such services need to be established to facilitate referrals, evaluations, interventions, and treatment. Like boys, especially teenage ones, girls are often un-likely to follow up on outside referrals, which makes it preferable to provide such services at the school itself or work with programs that have the capacity to go to the girls rather than waiting for them to show up, or more likely not show up. Too many opportunities to help are lost when the responsibility for follow-through is left solely on the shoulders of the girls themselves.

Communities that work most effectively are those where peo-ple make real efforts to build collaborations and where the collabo-rations take into account what is known about those in need. Much of what we have just described is built on this principle and will work well for teachers, schools, and parents and for the girls they all care about.

T: Talk and Listen

Talking and listening is as important at school as it is at home. Stu-dents need both adults willing to talk and listen to them one-on-one and opportunities for larger discussions.

Mentors. Studies that look at the factors that contribute most to the long-term success of girls clearly point to the great value of an adult mentor in girls' lives. It seems that this is even more impor-tant for girls than for boys, although it is a contributing factor for both. As has happened in many other efforts, much of the attention and investment has been directed to creating such opportunities for boys and less has been focused on girls, who have long been con-sidered resistant to many social risk factors. Yet in studies of suc-cessful women, including studies of successful women of color, the factor most commonly identified as important to their success was an adult who provided support, advice, encouragement, and opportunity. Whether this person was a parent, teacher, relative, neighbor, professional, or other individual seemed less important than the presence of someone who cares and shows interest. What did seem to matter was that this person be female, a role model with whom the other woman could identify.

Again, given the predominance of women teachers, schools provide great opportunities for girls to establish such key relationships. To help turn these opportunities into realities, school administrators need to recognize this mentoring role as one that teachers can fill and to value it as one of the things for which teachers are evaluated and rewarded. Teachers need to understand and value this role as part of their teaching and responsibility. At the same time, teachers need the skills to recognize when they may need to reach out to a student, and to recognize situations they may not be able to handle, knowing when to ask for help and when to involve other professionals. These abilities are intuitive for some but certainly not for all, and training may be required to maximize the effectiveness of supportive interactions and relationships.

Opportunities for Talking. Beyond possibilities for mentoring, schools can also create forums for discussing issues at a broader level. Teenagers, especially girls, benefit from talking about issues that they see as relevant to their lives. Forums on violence, violence prevention, tolerance, and respect can be very useful. Sometimes forums can be specifically related to an event that elevates everyone's concerns and anxiety, such as a school shooting elsewhere in the country. We found it perplexing when events such as the shootings at Columbine occurred and schools made a conscious decision not to create opportunities for students and teachers to talk about them. Such events require attention and talking, not silence and business as usual.

A local event can also be a good reason for talking—be it a fight, violence in the community, a newspaper story on high school hazing, or just about anything that comes to the attention of members of the school community. From such forums come opportunities for expressions of feeling and fears, as well as valuable ideas for what a school might do to avoid, prevent, or respond to an issue. Teachers and students bring their concerns and fears with them to school, and these can fester, potentially interfering with the learning process, or they can be vented and discussed, which may enhance the learning process.

Pulling It All Together

Schools can do a tremendous amount to model and teach prosocial skills and violence prevention behaviors. Schools can connect with parents and community resources to create prevention strategies and services, provide opportunities for mentoring, and encourage greater communication. All of these strategies are central to violence prevention but require special attention and consideration if they are to effectively address the issue of girls and violence. Given the relative newness of and inexperience with this issue, it is especially important to be creative, seek assistance from others, and take girls' different needs into consideration. Disregarding the new trends in girls' violence and school experiences with it is not a good idea, as the problem is not likely to just go away. Explaining this violence away or finding a reason to dismiss it as an unusual issue has been tried before, during the first two waves of the youth violence epidemic, and we all know the consequences of that approach. With that in mind, schools and teachers, with the involvement of parents, need to take this issue on and lead the way to making a serious effort to address girls' fighting proactively, before we are forced to confront this violence by some unthinkable tragedy.

Frequently Asked Questions

We are often asked about the role of schools in dealing with youth violence in general and violence among girls in particular. Here is what we are saying in response to some frequently asked questions.

1. How big a problem is bullying, and how can a school address bullying?

Bullying is a major issue for several reasons and certainly requires the attention of both parents and teachers. Over one-quarter of schoolchildren report in a range of surveys that they have experienced involvement in bullying as the bully or the bullied, or both. That alone would not necessarily be of great concern but for the fact that there are significant short- and long-term consequences that reflect social, educational, and behavioral dysfunction for all involved. Especially in the long term, there are issues that relate directly to the risk of involvement in violence. Those who bully have significantly higher rates as young adults of criminal behavior, violence, and social dysfunction. Those who have been bullied have significantly higher rates of mental health problems, specifically depression during adolescence and adulthood. Those who fall into both categories are particularly vulnerable; they are at high risk for the full range of long-term behavioral problems and have significant social and behavioral issues in the short term as well. Essentially, they need evaluation and help at the time the involvement in bullying is identified to address whatever may be going on then and to reduce their risk for future problems.

Punishment and exclusion of bullies is not the answer as these children may have a range of underlying issues including exposure to family violence, learning disabilities, and mental health issues. Those bullied cannot be ignored or dismissed as they may have issues that are contributing to the fact that they get singled out as targets for bullies, and they may need support, social skill development, and the like.

The more important role for schools, however, is that of broad-based prevention. Much work is being done in Europe and Scandinavia on bullying prevention. Leading researcher Daniel Olveus has developed simple strategies that are almost a cookbook, guiding schools in the development of bullying prevention programs that are relatively simple to implement and that create a broad cultural change in the school that really works.[3] Olveus has demonstrated dramatic declines in bullying, almost to the total elimination of the behavior, in numerous communities across Europe, and a growing number of schools in the United States are successfully replicating various versions of his approach. Very simply, it involves bringing all the stakeholders in the school community (students, teachers, administrators, parents) together to implement clear rules about respect and social interactions, good monitoring of behavior, role modeling by adults, educational curricula on tolerance and interpersonal interaction, and a reward system for desired behavior. Bullying is addressed with evaluation, behavioral change strategies, and maybe most important, a different response from peers than has been traditionally displayed. Often bullying is reinforced by peer reaction. It can be dramatically discouraged by lack of attention and lack of positive response from peers. Without a reinforcing audience, bullying loses its effect and appeal for the bully. It doesn't allow the bully to get what she wants, attention and status.

A key area for attention is the conscious inclusion of girls and their styles of bullying in the program and its educational elements. Girls can be subtle in the way they bully and especially at younger ages tend to use social exclusion, gossip, and physical threats as part of the process. Recognizing that this bullying is occurring requires a somewhat keener level of attention on the part of staff and often requires that the students themselves have input into identifying what is going on and with whom. Girls are likely to be aware of these situations long before adults are but need a safe and discreet way of passing on information, one that does not put them at risk.

Parents can be helpful by asking periodic questions about bullying at school or other places; girls may feel safer sharing their concerns and observations with parents or others outside of the school setting than with someone at school. It is very important, however, that parents ask not just if their own daughter is having problems but also if she is seeing bullying going on among others. This is one way that parents can begin to implement their commitment to play a parenting role with all children, not just their own.

2. How can schools set up a zero tolerance policy with constructive consequences?

As we say repeatedly, there is nothing wrong with, and in fact we strongly believe in, clear school policies that specify no tolerance for fighting, weapon carrying, drugs or alcohol, and the like, and that expect nothing less than respect for others and understanding and celebration of diversity and difference. All members of the school community need clarity about these expectations and all should be held accountable for a full commitment to these principles—students, teachers, administrators, staff, parents, and anyone else who enters the school for whatever reason.

Our concerns lie more with whether the consequences for violating these clear policies are constructive and educational or not and whether they are applied with consistency and equity. Students cannot have rules that some students are not held to; all must be treated equally and fairly. There have been unfortunate instances of some students being treated differently from others because of gender, race, or ethnicity. It is similarly confusing to students when they are governed by rules that they see being broken by adults in the school environment. Children and youths generally learn from what they see far more than from what they hear or read.

When serious rules are broken there should of course be serious consequences. But these behaviors are as much red flags for other problems as they are the breaking of a rule. Exclusion in the form of suspension or expulsion does not address these other problems. Schools can instead devise constructive options such as in-school suspension, required service to the school community (in other words, chores), learning projects, educational and psychosocial evaluation with appropriate therapy or treatment, involvement of parents, and so on. These are no different from the options that parents should consider when they must discipline their children.

It is crucial to remember that discipline should involve learning and need not be mean to make a point. In general, children and youths learn far better from constructive experiences than from punitive ones. Again, this by no means implies that rules can be broken without consequences or that the general safety of all in the school community is of anything less than the highest priority. It does mean that the consequences chosen need to be ones that actually teach and promote change for those directly involved as well as for all others who are watching what happens.

Girls and boys need to be treated in an equitable manner. There is a tendency to be harder on girls because gender stereotypes lead many to assume that girls should be held to higher standards, that it is normal to have higher expectations for them. There is a long-standing concern about the way girls are treated in the courts owing to higher expectations, and such inequity should not be replicated in other settings, such as schools.

In addition, girls and boys do learn differently, and consequences should be tailored to accommodate these differences. In general, girls tend to be more verbal than boys and should be allowed to express and explain themselves as much as possible—not so that they can explain away their behavior but so that underlying issues can be identified and addressed. Girls have higher rates of victim experiences, such as sexual abuse, dating violence, and the like, all of which can lead to acting-out behavior and all of which must be addressed if they are present. The long-term effects of these experiences, especially if left untreated, are extremely serious with respect to future victimization, violent behavior, criminal acts, and social dysfunction. What a sad statement a school makes about itself when a sexually abused teenage girl who is acting out is excluded or punished without ever being asked if something hurtful is going on in her life. In some ways this is not only adding another injury to the child but is telling her that whatever bad is happening to her is deserved or of no real concern.

3. What can parents do to encourage schools to address girls and violence? What role can parents play in the school process?

The very simple answer to this pair of questions is get involved in your daughter's school. Schools that have the active participation and involvement of parents tend to be better in all ways and are also more likely to include parents in planning, decision making, and problem solving.

With respect to girls and violence, it is important for parents to make sure that school leaders are aware of the changing dynamics in girls' behavior and recognize that they need to think about guiding girls' development and to implement programs to promote healthy and safe behavior. It is also important for parents to make sure that people who understand and know the specific needs of girls and the differences that must be considered are contributing to program and educational planning.

The best example is the importance of understanding the need to teach girls how to be both nonvictim and nonviolent. This teaching is not necessarily a simple task and is very different from teaching boys about violence prevention. It is never a good idea to merely apply strategies for boys to girls; it is always necessary to take a careful look at how that might play out. The juvenile justice system has for years dealt with girls by putting them into programs designed for boys and has experienced failure after failure as a result. Remarkably, it is only recently that the problem has been recognized, and efforts to correct it have only just begun. Schools must not follow this unhelpful path. Doing things the same old way with the same nonresults makes no sense.

4. What can teachers do to integrate violence prevention into their classroom?

There are many strategies for creating opportunities to address violence in the classroom. Packaged violence prevention and conflict resolution curricula are on the market; however, it is important to remember that many were developed with boys in mind, and they may or may not work well with girls or address girls' issues. Careful review is essential. Beyond this, depending on the class and the subject, ways of bringing the issue of violence prevention into learning activities include reading the newspaper in social studies; discussing essays, books, or short stories in English literature; writing about violence causes and prevention for English class; studying the biology of anger in health or science class; and so on. Any of these approaches not only incorporates the specific subject learning objectives but provides a venue for discussion and understanding of violence, the choices available, and the consequences of those choices. As violence and the fear of violence are such immediate issues for many children and most teenagers, it doesn't take much effort to engage them in taking the material they have read or written and applying it on a concrete level in their own lives.

Our experience is that kids want and need to talk about this, and we have even found that attendance improved in classes when violence prevention was the subject of a curriculum module. Especially for teenagers, a focus on topics and issues that they find relevant to their own lives greatly enhances their willingness to engage and learn. From our colleagues in teaching we have certainly learned that most teachers are highly aware of this but are often constrained by the materials they are required to use. Parents can again be helpful with this by working with teachers to ensure the flexibility that allows materials addressing issues relevant to their children to be available and incorporated into the classroom work.

5. How can partnerships be established to serve girls who are getting into trouble?

There are a number of ways of building partnerships and collaborations between schools and other public service organizations. One of the more common strategies is to establish school-based health centers that may initially offer basic health services but can over time expand to provide a broad range of services from mental health to nutrition to social services and outreach. School-based health programs are particularly valuable to girls, and the experience around the country is that girls often make up 75 to 80 percent of the student users. The health center becomes a nonacademic setting in which girls can share concerns and raise issues as well as receive preventive education on issues such as violence. Funding sources for these programs may involve both federal and private grants. Schools might start by developing relationships with some of the local medical professionals (doctors, nurses, and so on), involving them in health education classes or planning. Some of the existing clinics have started very small and built services over time; some have received considerable upfront funding and have offered an extensive range of services right from the start.

A second approach is to start small and involve other community-based professionals—people involved in mental health, youth outreach, and so on—in classes or career assemblies, and then build from these initial contacts. In some cases it is possible to install a modest presence of these services at the school; at other times, either because of financial or space limitations, the services remain in the community but are closely connected with the students through referrals and communications. Especially for teenagers, it is always best to bring services into the school, as students are then more likely to follow through on referrals and communication is far more reliable.

There is a growing movement around the country to think of school buildings as *multiservice centers* for children and youths. That is, the building is seen as a site where services and prevention programs can be consolidated, greatly improving access to and coordination of services and far better meeting the needs of students and their families.[4] Realizing this vision requires that school leaders be flexible and creative with both funding and space use. Parental involvement and support substantially helps schools in getting these visions off the ground, and parents are generally pleased with the results, as are the students. Teachers benefit greatly from such consolidations; they are no longer isolated from student services and

have far better access to help for students or just advice on how to
deal with issues.

6. What can school personnel do when students report violence in their homes?

It is inevitable that once violence prevention programs are set up
in a school, some students will identify themselves as children exposed to or experiencing violence in the home. Given the preva-
lence of domestic violence (possibly occurring in one-quarter to
one-third of families in all geographical and socioeconomic settings), it is likely that any given class has several students who are
witnessing or being subjected to violence in the home. This exposure is significant as it is a major risk factor for involvement in violence by these children as they grow up. Therefore it is essential
that teachers receive training in how to respond to these students
and have access to services as needed. In most states the identifica-
tion of child abuse requires teachers to report the situation to appropriate authorities. This is less true for the witnessing of domestic
violence, but it is essential that these exposed children receive
opportunities for counseling.

Links to community mental health services are central to
teachers' ability to respond appropriately and effectively. This
means that school leaders, with the support of parents, must for-
mally establish these links; otherwise teachers are left with difficult
situations and few means of addressing them. Teachers are neither
trained nor do they generally have the time to deal with this issue
alone and will be reluctant to address it without proper supports.

Indeed, no one discipline or sector of the community can deal
alone with the complex issues raised by any type of youth violence.
All need the professional relationships that make available the range
of skills required for both violence prevention and intervention.

Chapter Eight

What Communities Can Do

A number of years ago, Howard received a call from a friend for advice about something that had happened to her daughter. Maureen, a housewife and mother of two living with her family in a suburban neighborhood, was shopping one afternoon when an acquaintance came up to her saying, "You must be very proud of your daughter." Maureen had no idea what this was about but thanked her friend and went on with her shopping. Later that day she was picking up her son from school when she was again approached, this time by a neighbor who made a similar comment with the added statement, "You must be so excited about what happened."

At this point she realized that something was up and upon returning home immediately asked her daughter, Jessica, why people seemed to think she was proud and excited about something that had happened. Jessica, a middle school student, rather meekly, but with more than a bit of relish, told her mother that two boys had fought over her the previous day. Her ex-boyfriend had run into Jessica and her current boyfriend after school and had angrily called Jessica a "slut" for breaking up with him and starting to date this new boy. In reaction to this insult, Jessica's new boyfriend challenged him to a fight. Later that afternoon, the two boys, with a group of their friends totaling about sixty kids in all, gathered in a field by the railroad tracks where the boys fought it out with the crowd cheering and Jessica standing by.

Jessica claimed to be upset by what had happened, but her manner of telling the story made Maureen wonder if she had actually enjoyed being the center of attraction in this modern-day duel.

Maureen was further distressed that the story was spreading around the neighborhood and that the reaction of other adults and parents suggested that they thought such fighting was a good thing. What kind of values was this implying? What message was this sending to her daughter and the other kids in the community? What could or should she do about it?

At first, this story seemed to the two of us to be just one of many examples of the growing presence of violence in low-risk communities, a story that we would use to illustrate the second wave of the youth violence epidemic. Then, much more recently, we heard another story that was similar in its broadest outline but distinctly different in one major detail, the identities of the fighters.

Judy, a nurse and mother living in a Midwestern suburb, was driving home from work when she received a call on her cell phone from her daughter, Sophie, asking Judy to come down to the local police station to help her. Sophie and another girl from her school had been picked up by the police for fighting in the parking lot of the mall.

Sophie, a junior in high school, had been shopping after school with several of her friends when a classmate, who was also with several friends, came up to her and started pushing her around. The issue was that Sophie had started dating the former boyfriend of the other girl, who felt that Sophie was responsible for the breakup. The pushing escalated into a fistfight, with both girls getting cut and bruised and with various friends and other bystanders yelling louder and louder and encouraging the fighting. A passing police cruiser stopped, broke up the fight, and brought the girls to the station in order to get the parents involved.

The girls were charged with disorderly conduct, although these charges were later dropped. The parents of both girls were rather distressed, and no one could figure out quite what to do or how to respond or where to go for help.

These two stories in combination reflect the changing dynamics of the roles girls play in violence, and both raise issues of what girls, parents, and communities need to do to address the problem of girls' violence from a preventive perspective rather than just responding after fights have occurred. Jessica's experience occurred at a time when girls were involved in violence most often as victims or as objects of a conflict between two boys. Sophie's more recent experience exemplifies the new dynamic where girls are the aggressors and where boys are the objects of the conflict. Girls are fighting like boys, and communities, the second circle of influence around individuals (as illustrated earlier in Figure 4.1), have an important role to play in addressing this.

Furthermore, parents can and need to bring the problem of violence to the forefront of community agendas. They must also ensure that their daughters are viewed in a positive and constructive manner in the public debate and in the design and implementation of prevention and service initiatives. Communities need to move from a reactive stance to a protective agenda. The story of a real community we'll call Springfield illustrates the learning that one town has had to go through to make this move.

Springfield, USA, was a small city that had evolved from a suburb but still had a largely suburban quality and style of life. Life in Springfield was relatively uneventful until several decades ago when the city began to experience problems with several gangs that had developed among its high school students. Some thought that gangs had spread to Springfield from the big city ninety miles away. These gangs were all made up of boys. The town had responded with a number of programs involving the police, health care professionals, religious leaders, and parent groups that had successfully addressed this problem, with life returning to its previous quiet and calm. Then the problem resurfaced, but this time in the form of the development of two groups of girls who were displaying the aggressive, territorial, violent behaviors that had been seen earlier with the boys.

The community was caught off guard. There was a long period of disbelief and denial about what was happening. Excuses were made to explain away the graffiti, acts of vandalism, episodes of petty theft, and fights that were beginning to occur. It was just hard to believe that girls were acting this way. Local experts, drawn from the college in the community, found that the limited research on girls focused on girls as victims and the unfair treatment of girls in the criminal justice system. So the episodes were characterized as aberrations, overreactions, and examples of how girls were harshly labeled for behaviors that boys would never be criticized for. Boys could be boys, but girls could not be bad and were being made to suffer just because social expectations did not allow for such misbehavior. The community and its experts chose to stick their heads in the ground, as if the problem were an illusion that would evaporate.

Not surprisingly, the problem did not evaporate. The violence and criminal behavior increased, with several girls ending up in court and in the state juvenile justice system. Finally, the city was forced to pull its head up and respond. Programs used in quelling the previous crisis were reinstituted with a focus on girls, but the outcomes were not nearly as successful. Although they were making a difference, it was neither dramatic nor adequate enough, and in fact, several more groups of girls were beginning to form, modeling themselves after the original two groups.

After an extensive effort to bring all the stakeholders in the city together, and with an aggressive effort on the part of some parents in the community, people realized that the city needed to respond with increased attention to whatever factors lay behind this new dynamic, and they even began to consider bringing the girls themselves into the process and making them part of the solution.

Now there is a comprehensive effort in Springfield that includes all the players from the earlier crisis with boys and also involves girls, parents, and professionals who bring special expertise in girls. Although the problem is far from resolved, violent incidents are declining, and the girls' groups are moving toward more prosocial activities and behaviors.

We wonder what might have happened in Springfield if this more comprehensive developmental and gender-specific approach had been created and implemented sooner, when the first signs of a problem emerged. We also certainly wonder why when girls are involved, there is such a tendency toward denial, excuses, and disbelief. Girls are different from boys, just not that different!

Applying the ART Model to Communities

There are many levels, from national to neighborhood, on which we could approach the topic of community action with respect to girls and violence. Here we will focus primarily on the local community level, as this is the point at which parents, families, teachers, and others can make the greatest difference in girls' immediate environment. However, this focus in no way precludes the importance of also addressing girls' risk and resiliency. Issues such as media messages; broad national values that promote violence as a problem solver; behaviors and actions of the juvenile justice system; national policies affecting education, handgun availability, and youth development are certainly not minor and require action. But this action requires parents, educators, and community leaders to join with state and national advocacy efforts, and we believe that state and national efforts can be most effectively influenced by action and success at the local level. In other words, your best strategy may be to start at a place where you can make a real difference and then to apply the experience gained from that effort to the larger national violence prevention movement. Nothing speaks louder than success.

The core principle underlying community efforts is that everyone has a role in and a responsibility for the health and safety of all girls in the community. Some roles are big and some small, but everyone has one. Those involved are essentially building on the concept that it takes a village to make a difference in the lives of the children of the community. No one can do it alone; individual parents need help and support in order to create an environment around their daughters that promotes prosocial values and healthy, safe development.

A: Act as a Role Model

Just as girls need healthy role models in the home and at school, they need to see the values and behaviors that support these healthy roles in their community as well. All members of the community need to consider how their own personal actions influence the children around them. Demonstrating tolerance and respect for others, modeling nonviolent conflict resolution, and constructively dealing with anger and frustration all set a tone in the community that can have great impact on how children and youths behave. This is true about the ways people conduct themselves when driving their cars, interacting with others in stores and supermarkets, having casual encounters on the sidewalk, or taking part in pretty much any of the general daily activities in the community. All of us get angry, but we make choices about how we express that anger or try to resolve our frustrations. The words we use, the body language we express, and the resolutions we desire all give out important messages. Being nice is not always easy, but trying to be so is always a better behavior to model than is jumping to an aggressive approach.

When someone gets angry or frustrated, rather than responding to anger with anger, the better response can be saying something like, "What would you like me to do?" or, "What would you like to happen?" This works at home and can work in just about any interaction in the community. Consistent and positive efforts can teach kids a style of behavior that reduces the likelihood of conflict and increases the chance of a good outcome. If this approach is to be broadly effective, it requires a community-wide commitment to displaying the behaviors community members want their children to learn and use.

R: Reach Out to Others

Reaching out to others is probably the most important component of the ART model at the community level. It requires that all community stakeholders not only take on responsibility for the children of the community but also join in a broad community effort to work together to influence the community environment.

Obviously, the roles that people play in reaching out can vary greatly, but whether it is large or small, all participation and involvement is crucial as it is the collective effort that makes the real difference. Larger institutions such as schools, churches, and the police have larger roles as they need to develop programs that engage girls in activities that create safe environments and offer prosocial learning and positive experiences as well as structured settings to minimize the amount of free time, which is when girls are most likely to get into trouble.

But individuals do things that are equally important. The mother who opens up her house after school as a place with an adult presence where her daughter and her daughter's friends can hang out is essentially parenting all of the girls; she is an extension of all the parents of the girls in the group. The grandmother who sits out on her porch as girls are walking home from school and talks with some of them and asks simple questions is demonstrating caring and interest that does not go unnoticed or unappreciated. The storeowner who allows her store to be a place for hanging out or even makes an effort to employ some of the girls is extending the parenting role beyond the family. The community employer who creates opportunities for girls to contribute to the community is giving them a chance to feel like valued members of that community, and young people need not just to be taken care of but also to feel that they bring something to the benefit of others. The teacher or police officer who helps to organize after-school activities such as sports, a community cleanup, or an ongoing project such as routinely visiting patients in a hospital or nursing home is not only modeling caring behavior but giving girls meaningful community involvement. The list of possibilities is endless. All of these little things add up to a widespread environment that provides nurturing, opportunity, mentoring, modeling, and meaning for girls and young women who are struggling for identity and value.

Girls also need opportunities to earn money and feel successful. Community-wide efforts to identify jobs, from babysitting to after-school employment, are extremely important, both to fill girls' free time and to create a connection between being responsible and being successful. In many communities, efforts such as these often focus on boys, as they are the ones seen as likely to get into trouble. Girls can no longer be left out of this effort, and in fact many work opportunities may be more appropriate for or of more interest to girls. There is a great need to give girls and boys equal access to work and opportunities to make community contributions.

For responding effectively to girls who are already getting into trouble or are seen as at risk, coordination and collaboration among the various community services is essential. Like school services, community services in areas such as physical health, mental health, education, juvenile justice, and youth programs need to be linked as seamlessly as possible. Girls do not travel between services any more reliably than boys do. Putting the necessity of making such links onto the girls themselves is unlikely to result in success. Services need to be linked and connected in ways that minimize the need for the girls themselves to tie everything together, because that just won't happen.

T: Talk and Listen

In the communications arena, the real emphasis is on listening. Kids need to feel heard and respected at the community level. Girls in particular need to feel they have a voice in the community—that their opinions and ideas are sought out, heard, and valued. Community leaders (in city hall, town hall, or neighborhood citizen groups) need to ensure girls are included. It takes little effort to make sure that some young women are identified and recruited into community planning and leadership. Not only will they bring good ideas but they will attract other youths into community projects and efforts. Leaders have considerably better credibility among the young when youths are included in leadership activities. This approach also models inclusion and demonstrates the value a community places on its children.

Parent Advocacy

The role of parents as advocates for their daughters is key to carrying out the ART model in the community. Parents need to stand up and require that community leaders bring their daughters into the process and create the programs and opportunities that better ensure the success of their daughters. Given the opportunity, girls will step up and show their value, but adults need to open the door and hold community leaders responsible and accountable for this to happen.

It is also important, as mentioned earlier, for parents to get involved with broader advocacy efforts involving national policy. None of us can expect increases in resources for youth, reductions in access to handguns, increased accountability among the media for the messages and values they promote, or changes in juvenile justice programs so that they recognize the unique aspects and needs of girls unless we put pressure on state and national policymakers. The reality is that children and youths are generally at the bottom of the list of priorities in government. After all, children don't vote, and their issues rarely rise to the top of the concerns and priorities identified in political polls. This is sad but true, and whether we like it or not, this puts the burden and the responsibility on parents and those who care about children and youths to be the voice that changes this reality. Superimposed on this is a second reality—the needs of girls are generally on the low end of the priority scale even among children's issues. Boys make more noise and therefore get more attention. How else is it that we have a juvenile justice system that puts most of its resources into programs for boys? How else is it that most of the youth development resources are targeted to boys? Do we need to wait until girls make the same noise as boys before we acknowledge the need to invest in their future? Many parents and teachers certainly hope not.

Frequently Asked Questions

Here are three issues that people raise with us about community involvement in their daughters' lives.

1. *What can parents do to influence the level of attention paid to girls and violence?*

Girls need a voice in the community and need to be on community leaders' radar screens with respect to the attention given to violence prevention and general safety. This generally does not happen without the voice of their parents to open doors so that girls are noticed and included. Girls just aren't on community radar screens except when it comes to long-standing issues primarily related to teen pregnancy prevention and girls as victims of violence. Acknowledgment of the increase in violent behavior among girls is generally slow until something drastic happens. Even when there is a crisis, a typical reaction is to deny, make excuses, and explain away the situation, as happened in Springfield, USA. Parents must be advocates for their children, and as girls are generally seen as nonthreatening (that "sugar and spice" thing), little will happen without some effort.

There is a second group of community members who can be enlisted to help individual parents or groups of parents push the issue—survivors. Survivors, parents who have lost a child to violence and others who have suffered the pain of violence, have been a powerful voice in the violence prevention movement across the country. Many of the survivors involved in advocacy are women and mothers. All of them bring a real face to the issue as well as passion and serious motivation for action and change.

Our own experience in Boston has taught us that trying to start by appealing to the top, to the political leaders of the community, for change and action is difficult and frustrating. It is better to start within a neighborhood and bring together the key neighborhood stakeholders, both to share information and concern and to take some small steps at this very local level. A few sympathetic teachers, community residents, health and mental health providers, parents, survivors (if they are available), and maybe some teen girls can create a critical mass of energy to get something started and to reach out to enlist others in a growing effort to create understanding, visibility, and movement.

It is hard to do this alone. Working with even a few friends, possibly the parents of your daughter's friends with whom you have already started to connect around some of your parenting efforts, can make a huge difference in speaking out. The early work in Boston in preventing boys' violence, including homicide, involved only a handful of people. We often met in church basements and similar places with only a few people showing up. But in time this changed, and ultimately, hundreds if not thousands of people got involved. Even the political leaders eventually got on board. It takes patience, persistence, and commitment, but this effort is worth it and makes a difference for your children.

2. What can teachers do?

Along with parents, teachers are natural and credible advocates for children and need to be heard and involved. Many teachers speak both as women and mothers and as professionals and experts in teaching. More often than not they are also the ones who are witnessing firsthand the changes that are occurring, and can put a real and personal face on the issue. This in turn increases the ability of others to relate to the problem and to engage in action and concern.

Much of the approach for teachers is very similar to that for parents, and the combination of parents and teachers should be used wherever possible because it is so helpful for creating a critical mass of energy and establishing a highly credible and committed group at the core of the building process.

3. What are ways of joining in broader national efforts?

The best way to join in large-scale advocacy efforts is to find an existing group, such as the Children's Defense Fund, or to look for local-level groups like yours in other communities and work with them to build a broader geographical base. If you go the route of working with an existing national organization, contact the organization to find out what you can do to help or how you can organize a local chapter or group. It is important to do some research beforehand to assure yourself that the group is legitimate and is guided by values and concerns that fit with your own. Searching the Internet or making queries of friends or local resources can help you with this research. Going the route of building an effort by finding others with similar concerns and community-level efforts is probably more difficult and certainly slower but not at all impossible or futile. Mothers Against Drunk Driving (MADD) is a great example of how powerful such an approach can be, as this originally community-level effort was central in changing national attitudes, laws, and behavior and has possibly been more influential than any other group dealing with the issue of drunk driving.

A network of parent and sibling survivor groups representing communities around the country already exists. This network is growing, and it is taking the issue of youth violence prevention to a higher and more visible level. A coalition of parent groups and survivor groups could be a successful effort, along the lines of MADD, if sufficient energy and effort were invested. It is certainly worth a try.

Chapter Nine

A Call to Action

As a physician, Deborah was seeing patients in the adolescent clinic at a health center in Dorchester, Massachusetts, when a mother brought her fourteen-year-old daughter, Sandra, in for a routine physical. Sandra's very attentive mother wanted to stay for the initial interview, which the clinic allowed (many questions would be asked a second time once her mother left the room). Because of the growing attention to violence prevention at the health center, "Have you been in a fight recently?" had become one of the screening questions asked of teens. When Deborah asked this of Sandra the first time, with her mother present, Sandra became quite animated. She readily described a recent fight between her group of girls and a woman on a bus. With a palpable sense of pride and only a bit of embarrassment, Sandra provided the details.

Sandra and her girlfriends were riding in the back of the bus and sharing a cigarette. A woman, whom Sandra said was drinking alcohol, called out to her, saying, "Bitch, put out that cigarette." Sandra was insulted and did not put out the cigarette. Once again the woman repeated the insult. Sandra said that she and her friends were furious. So when the woman got off the bus, the group of girls got off too and beat her up quite badly. Not surprisingly stunned, by the story itself as well as the fact that Sandra told all of this in front of her mother, Deborah turned to the mother for some reaction. Sandra's mother's response was a somewhat indignant, "Well, you wouldn't let anyone call you that name would you?" Deborah's shock and concern were multiplied with this response. Perhaps the mother was so embarrassed by what her daughter had done that she could think of nothing else to say. Perhaps the mother felt a bit of pride that her daughter had stood up for herself and wasn't a wimp. Sandra's mother understood that fighting was wrong, but letting someone insult you in public without responding was even more wrong in her book. Needless to say, this visit with Sandra and her mother turned out to be considerably longer than the usual routine visit, with a prolonged conversation addressing the implications and risks of such behavior. The discussion focused on how Sandra's mother might help Sandra develop a list of options for responding to such situations. Ultimately, Sandra was referred to the violence prevention counselor at the clinic.

What Deborah really wished was that she could refer the mother, and the whole community for that matter, to a violence prevention counselor.

Certainly, no parent wants a wimp for a child. That has been made clear to us over and over again by parents all over the country. It is not just poor inner-city parents in high violent crime areas who are telling their children to stand up for themselves and go back outside and fight to ensure respect and not allow themselves to be pushed around. Another such story Deborah often shares is that of a colleague whose child played ice hockey. A fight started between this child and another child during one game, and the latter wanted to continue it on a corner field in their neighborhood, an upper-class Boston suburb. After several phone calls to the house, taunting his child to come to the designated spot and finish the fight, Deborah's colleague (a physician) told his son to go with his brother and beat up the other kid. In fact the father gave very specific advice to his son, "Walk right up to him and punch him out. Don't spend any time talking." Evidently, the fight did happen. His son won, and all the kids involved are best friends now.

No one wants a wimp for a child. Or better said, parents don't want anyone to take advantage of their children. We understand this, and this is often especially true of girls. However, there is tremendous irony in the fact that parents often allow or even encourage children to do things in the name of self-defense and respect that actually increase the risk of harm to a child. Certainly a child like Sandra might ignore an insult from a drinking woman on a bus. Certainly a father might protect his son or daughter from a corner fight by helping the child figure out what else he or she could do to defuse a situation like a fight during a sports event. What if one of the kids waiting at the corner field had been carrying a knife or a gun? What if someone had been badly hurt in this fight that had been endorsed by this physician father?

Without the social support of a nonviolent community that values negotiation, compromise, forgiveness, and other conflict resolution skills, it becomes ever harder for parents to raise nonviolent children. This is where the entertainment media, the schools, and the larger society all have a role and are important stakeholders in supporting parents in the raising of safe and healthy children. Think back to those concentric circles presented earlier in Figure 4.1 and their influence on your child. All the layers that surround your child—family, peers, school, community—need to line up to promote safe and healthy values and deemphasize or discourage risky and dangerous behaviors. Your actions and efforts to raise your child have to also include creating a supportive community and recognizing that you as an individual parent cannot do this alone.

Personal Reflections: Caught off Guard

Over a decade ago, when the first questions related to girls and violence began to pop up at our presentations, we were caught off guard. Not that we hadn't thought about girls before in our work, but our focus had been based on our impressions that girls were part of the youth violence epidemic in two specific ways—as victims (dating violence, sexual abuse, domestic violence) and as instigators and bystanders. We were mainly advocates for programs that imparted to girls skills to prevent and avoid victimization, essentially empowerment programs, and that imparted to boys a set of values and attitudes about respect and standards for dating relationships. In addition we recognized that girls need to understand the roles they play as encouraging bystanders when fights take place and the potential risky consequences of making boyfriends jealous or in other ways setting up situations that may lead to boys fighting. We still believe these strategies are important, but things have gotten more complicated.

What caught us off guard were the new experiences that school personnel (teachers and principals) were sharing with us about girls as aggressors and in particular girls fighting girls. These were new to us. There were few data reflecting these trends, and we monitored trends in violence rather closely, to be prepared for the questions and reports about the evolving behavior among girls. Like most experts in the field of violence prevention, we thought that girls, through socialization and maybe biology, were protected from or resilient to the toxic environment that promoted violence among boys.

Even though we were aware of the increasing proportion of girls involved with the juvenile justice system for violent crime, we had bought into the explanations of juvenile justice academicians, the experts, that this was a reflection of the different and biased manner in which girls were treated by the police, courts, and juvenile justice system.

Little Information Available

After both of us had been challenged several times by questions and comments from audiences about girls and violence, we began to wonder what was behind what we were hearing. We had learned from our experience with the growth of youth violence in suburbia that individual experiences, especially similar reports made in multiple settings, could be early warning signs of something new developing. So we hit the books, the scientific and professional journals, and the Internet for information and answers.

However, we found very little to help us. There were almost no data to substantiate a rise in girl-on-girl violence. There was no specific evidence that reflected a change in toxic environmental risk factors that could explain or advance our understanding of what might be behind a behavioral change among girls. No one was writing about girls as aggressors. The writing about girls was entirely focused on girls and self-destructive behavior (eating disorders, self-mutilation, depression and suicide, underachievement in science and other traditionally male arenas) and girls as victims. Emphasis was on empowerment to address and reduce victimization and on the dangerous and inappropriate role models that promoted unhealthy eating behaviors and body image perceptions. Not that this information was unimportant, but it did not help us respond to what we were hearing. Girls fighting girls was just not on the radar screen, and most of what we could find, even books covering a broad spectrum of girls' issues, had no mention of girls committing violence.

Lessons from Our Daughters

The two of us began to talk about this issue increasingly often, bouncing hypotheses and perspectives off each other. What was different?

Ultimately, it was talking about our own daughters and thinking open-endedly about our observations of them that began to shed light on our thinking. It was through our daughters that we were exposed to the dramatic shift in the female role models being presented in the media. This shift had been subtle at first but was beginning to progress more rapidly. As we discussed earlier, it had started with what appeared to be relatively benign characters like the Pink Power Ranger but then evolved into far less subtle images of supersheroes and violent villainesses—on TV, in movies, in video games, in magazines. Howard in particular had observed that his daughter was drawn only to those TV action shows where girls were part of the group of heroic characters. Deborah was also hearing comments from her daughter that reflected a similar attraction to these TV characters. Neither of our daughters was aggressive in her behavior, so it was more upon reflection that we took a closer look at something that had seemed innocuous at first. We became increasingly convinced that this shift might have the potential to change how girls were behaving. As hard as we tried, we could not identify another cultural shift that we could comfortably tie into the mix.

Knowing how powerful the media were as an educational influence and a promoter of values among children, we starting sharing this perspective with others. We began to test it out with colleagues and friends. We also began to talk about it in our public presentations and in response to questions about girls. Not surprisingly, the initial reactions were far from supportive, maybe even a little amused. The Pink Power Ranger? How could we think that the Pink Power Ranger was responsible for girls' fighting?

Are We Being Alarmists?

Had we gone off the deep end on this? This was a question we asked ourselves repeatedly. But the questions and concerns about fighting among girls kept coming, and not just from teachers. We began getting similar comments from parents and other community residents, and when we talked to groups of students in schools, we started hearing of incidents from young people as well. We could not ignore this, nor could we find other underlying risk factors that had changed for girls.

Friends and colleagues began to send us other material—fashion spreads from upscale teen magazines entitled, "Who wants to be nice anymore?" with models looking like gang members holding machine guns and ammunition belts. Newspaper stories about high school and college sororities using violent hazing methods, sometimes more scary than reports about fraternity hazing, began to appear. The percentage of arrests of juvenile girls for violent crimes continued to rise. Ads for gun ownership from gun manufacturers started appearing that were clearly targeting women, especially young women, as a new market. All of this enhanced our own level of concern, and we experienced growing acceptance, or at the very least growing consideration, of our perspective and ideas.

And no, we are not trying to be alarmist. We are trying to alert everyone, especially parents, to the risks and the consequences of these risks that are beginning to play out, in the hope that this wave of youth violence can be addressed more proactively than the first two waves of this epidemic were. Girls still represent a very small part of the problem and are an even smaller part of the more serious violence that this country is experiencing. Now is the time to take action, not after things get worse and the solutions become far more difficult and expensive in both human and financial costs.

Parents and Teachers Must Take Action

We strongly believe that the leadership for changing the toxic environment affecting girls and violence must come from parents and that parents must be helped and supported in this by teachers and schools. You who are parents, teachers, and school administrators and other personnel are the ones on the front line, and you are the ones who can have the greatest impact on the immediate experiences and environments of girls. You are the role models, the teachers of values and behaviors, and the closest in terms of being invested in the consequences. You are the ones who can ultimately have the greatest impact on public policy and on the corporate behavior of the media, advertising, and Internet industries. You cannot do it alone, but you can make a difference in the lives of this nation's daughters and in the attitudes of its elected leaders.

When we look at the successful responses to violence among boys in inner cities and then in the more affluent suburbs, we see that the role of parents and schools has been crucial in affecting change in local communities and at the national level. It is more important than ever to replicate this approach now for girls, when it is early in the process and we all have the best chance of changing things before worst-case scenarios begin to play out.

Tips for All

To this end we close with a brief set of key suggestions for parents, teachers, and schools. They summarize the most important concepts and actions presented in this book, the ones all of us should stay focused on.

1. Even though girls are still a small part of the big picture in terms of the most serious violence, there is clear evidence that this is changing, and the status quo will not hold much longer.

2. Parents are the teachers of values and behavior for their daughters and must always keep in mind that their daughters are learning from what they see. *The "A" in the ART of parenting is to act as a role model.*

3. Parents cannot teach values and behavior alone and must build a community around their daughters that supports the development of healthy and safe behavior. *The "R" in the ART of parenting is to reach out to others, create a parenting support network for your daughter.*

4. Support networks should include extended family and family friends as well as the parents of your daughter's friends, establishing a sense of group responsibility in the raising of a community's daughters.

5. It is essential to maintain ongoing communication with your daughter, even through the rough times. *The "T" in the ART of parenting is to talk and listen, with an emphasis on listening.*

6. Finding opportunities for conversation gets increasingly difficult as girls enter the middle to late teenage years, and parents need to be creative in encouraging these interactions. Use the in-the-car or a similar strategy, and be alert to the times when your daughter seems to be open to talking and sharing; make an effort to replicate these positive circumstances whenever possible.

7. Even when it is difficult to tell your daughter what she should do, you can always share with her what you will do or how you will feel if she makes certain choices. You cannot always control her, but you can always control yourself and how you will react.

8. Teachers and schools play an important role in the raising of girls and need to recognize the increase in girls' violence and respond accordingly. Adapt the ART of parenting model to the school setting with respect to modeling behavior and values, teaching skills that affect behavior, reaching out to build a community within and around the school in a multi-service center approach, and creating opportunities for talking and listening that allow girls to express themselves and feel like valued members of the school community.

9. Zero-tolerance policies that exclude students are not effective and cause schools to miss important opportunities to help girls in trouble and keep girls engaged. Creative discipline that includes in-school suspensions, comprehensive evaluations and interventions, school and community services, and involvement of appropriate professionals needs to be standard.

10. Parents and teachers have to play an active role in community change because there is no one else likely to step up to speak to the needs of girls in the community.

11. Similarly, parents and teachers need to join in the larger efforts to promote national public policies that recognize the needs of girls and ensure that adequate resources are committed for violence prevention and services for girls.

12. Together, we can make a difference!

Remember, girls are different! And then again, they are proving to be not *that* different. There is still time to heed Leonard Eron's advice and socialize both our boys and girls more as we used to socialize our girls. Skills that help both boys and girls with being nice, compromising, negotiating, empathizing, and resolving conflict must be taught, practiced, and made popular.

As in our last book we close with our prayers and hopes—this time for the girls and young women of this country. They deserve adults' most dedicated efforts, and *together, all of us can make a difference*.

Notes

Chapter One

1. Lizzie Borden, a woman living with her parents in Fall River, Massachusetts, murdered both her mother and father with an ax on August 4, 1892.
2. In 1969, Charles Manson broke into two homes in California and murdered the families and visitors who were there. He was accompanied by four women who assisted with the murders and then defended Charles Manson.
3. Rosalind Wiseman, author of *Queen Bees and Wannabes: Helping Your Daughter Survive Cliques, Gossip, Boyfriends, and Other Realities of Adolescence* (New York: Three Rivers Press, 2002), labels this behavior as building alliances. It relates directly to Queen Bees' need for group support and backup.
4. Federal Bureau of Investigation, Uniform Crime Reports, www.fbi.gov/ucr/ucr.htm, 2003.
5. This is a story that Deborah's husband, Reverend Charles Stith, uses in Sunday morning sermons.

Chapter Two

1. For further discussion of these waves, see D. Prothrow-Stith and H. R. Spivak, *Murder Is No Accident: Understanding and Preventing Youth Violence in America* (San Francisco: Jossey-Bass, 2004), pp. 18–20.

2. S. Sandler (ed.), *Ophelia Speaks* (New York: HarperCollins, 1999), p. 283, Appendix B.

3. Leonard Eron, Ph.D., an American psychologist who has conducted longitudinal studies of children, aggression, and behavioral influences in upstate New York, often lectures on the role of socialization in children's violent behavior. We heard him make this comment at a Youth Violence Prevention and Agenda-Setting conference at the Harvard School of Public Health, Boston, 1993.

4. U.S. Department of Justice, Bureau of Justice Statistics, "Homicide Trends in the U.S.: Intimate Homicide," www. ojp.usdoj. gov/bjs/homicide/intimates.htm, 2004; J. Weiler, "An Overview of Research on Girls and Violence," CHOICES Brief no. 1 (New York: Teachers College, Institute for Urban and Minority Education, 1999); M. Chesney-Lind, "Girls' Crime and Woman's Place," *Crime and Delinquency*, 1989, 35(1), 5–29.

5. C. D. Ness, "Why Girls Fight: Female Youth Violence in the Inner City," *Annals of the American Academy of Political and Social Science*, 2004, pp. 32–48.

6. M. Talbot, "Mean Girls and the New Movement to Tame Them," *New York Times Magazine*, Feb. 24, 2002, pp. 24–29, 40, 58, 64–65.

7. R. Wiseman, *Queen Bees and Wannabes: Helping Your Daughter Survive Cliques, Gossip, Boyfriends, and Other Realities of Adolescence* (New York: Three Rivers Press, 2002).

8. R. Simmons, *Odd Girl Out: The Hidden Culture of Aggression in Girls* (New York: Harcourt, 2002).

9. For more information on this program, visit www.empowered. org.

10. P. Chesler, *Woman's Inhumanity to Woman* (New York: Penguin, 2003).

11. F. Adler, *Sisters in Crime* (New York: McGraw-Hill, 1975), pp. 31–53.

12. Adler, *Sisters in Crime*, pp. 85–110.

Chapter Three

1. See, for example, Federal Bureau of Investigation, www.fbi.gov/publications.htm.
2. See, for example, National Institute of Justice, www.nij.ncjrs.org/publications/pubs_db.asp.
3. See, for example, Centers for Disease Control and Prevention, www.cdc.gov/ncipc/pub-res/research_agenda/09_youthviolence.htm.
4. Centers for Disease Control and Prevention, "Homicide Among Young Black Men," *Morbidity and Mortality Weekly Reports*, Oct. 18, 1985.
5. J. C. Barancik and others, "Northeast Ohio Trauma Study," *American Journal of Public Health*, 1983, 73, 746–751.
6. U.S. Department of Justice, Office of Juvenile Justice and Delinquency Prevention, "Juvenile Justice: A Century of Changes," 1999 National Report Series (Washington, D.C.: U.S. Department of Justice, 1999), pp. 1–4.
7. Federal Bureau of Investigation, Uniform Crime Reports, www.fbi.gov/ucr/ucr.htm, 2003.
8. U.S. Department of Justice, Office of Juvenile Justice and Delinquency Prevention, pp. 1–4.
9. Girls Incorporated, "Girls and Violence," Fact Sheet, www.girls-inc.org, May 2001.
10. Federal Bureau of Investigation, "Most Wanted," www.fbi.gov/mostwant.htm.
11. Federal Bureau of Investigation, Uniform Crime Reports, www.fbi.gov/ucr/ucr.htm, 2003.
12. Centers for Disease Control and Prevention, Youth Risk Behavior Surveillance System (YRBSS), http://www.cdc.gov/yrbss.
13. M. Feldman, D. Prothrow-Stith, and T. Chery, "Homicide Survivors: Research and Practice Implications," *Journal of Preventive Medicine*, special supplement, forthcoming.

Chapter Four

1. D. Prothrow-Stith and H. R. Spivak, *Murder Is No Accident: Understanding and Preventing Youth Violence in America* (San Francisco: Jossey-Bass, 2004).

2. M. Feldman, D. Prothrow-Stith, and T. Chery, "Homicide Survivors: Research and Practice Implications," *Journal of Preventive Medicine*, special supplement, forthcoming.

3. A. L. Kellerman and others, "Gun Ownership as a Risk Factor for Homicide in the Home," *New England Journal of Medicine*, 1993, *329*, 1084–1091.

4. J. H. Sloan and others, "Handgun Regulations, Crime, Assaults, and Homicide: A Tale of Two Cities," *New England Journal of Medicine*, 1988, *319*, 1256–1262.

5. American Correctional Association, *The Female Offender: What Does the Future Hold?* (Lanham, Md.: American Correctional Association, 1990).

6. U.S. Department of Justice, Office of Juvenile Justice and Delinquency Prevention, *Guiding Principles for Promising Female Programming: An Inventory of Best Practices* (Washington, D.C.: U.S. Department of Justice, Oct. 1998).

7. L. Acoca and K. Dedel, *No Place to Hide: Understanding and Meeting the Needs of Girls in the California Juvenile Justice System* (San Francisco: National Council on Crime and Delinquency, 1998).

8. C. S. Widom, "Does Violence Beget Violence? A Critical Examination of the Literature," *Psychological Bulletin*, 1989, *106*, 3–28.

9. M. Chesney-Lind, J. Koo, D. Kata, and K. Fujiwara, *Girls at Risk: An Overview of Gender-Specific Programming Issues and Initiatives*, Report no. 394 (Honolulu: University of Hawaii, Social Sciences Research Institute, Center for Youth Research, 1998).

10. D. B. Sugarman and G. T. Hotaling, "Dating Violence: A Review of Contextual and Risk Factors," in B. Levy (ed.), *Dating Violence: Young Women in Danger* (Seattle: Seal Press, 1991).

11. Centers for Disease Control and Prevention, Morbidity and Mortality Weekly Report Surveillance Summaries, May 21, 2004, vol. 53, no. SS-2, p. 8. www.cdc.gov/mmwr/PDF/SS/SS5302.pdf.

12. Chesney-Lind, Koo, Kata, and Fujiwara, *Girls at Risk.*

13. Chesney-Lind, Koo, Kata, and Fujiwara, *Girls at Risk.*

14. J. P. Tierney, J. B. Grossman, and N. L. Resch, *Making a Difference: An Impact Study of Big Brothers/Big Sisters* (Philadelphia: Public/Private Ventures, 1995).

15. C. Gilligan, *In a Different Voice: Psychological Theory and Women's Development* (Cambridge, Mass.: Harvard University Press, 1982).

16. S. Artz, *Sex, Power, and the Violent School Girl* (New York: Teachers College Press, 1999); see the chapter titled "Exploring Theories of Female Crime and Delinquency," pp. 1–25.

17. U.S. Department of Justice, Office of Juvenile Justice and Delinquency Prevention, *Guiding Principles for Promising Female Programming.*

18. U.S. Department of Justice, Office of Juvenile Justice and Delinquency Prevention, *Guiding Principles for Promising Female Programming.*

19. K. H. Federle and M. Chesney-Lind, "Special Issues in Juvenile Justice: Gender, Race, and Ethnicity," in I. M. Schwartz (ed.), *Juvenile Justice and Public Policy: Toward a National Agenda* (New York: Maxwell-Macmillan, 1992).

20. American Correctional Association, *The Female Offender.*

Chapter Five

1. J. Garbarino, *Raising Children in a Socially Toxic Environment* (San Francisco: Jossey-Bass, 1995).

2. C. W. Turner, B. W. Hesse, and S. Peterson-Lewis, "Naturalistic Studies of the Long Term Effects of Television Violence," *Journal of Social Issues,* 1986, pp. 51–73.

3. J. Garbarino, *Lost Boys: Why Our Sons Turn Violent and How We Can Save Them* (New York: Free Press, 1999).

4. S. Bok, *Mayhem: Violence as Public Entertainment* (Reading, Mass.: Addison-Wesley, 1998).

5. C. D. Ness, "Why Girls Fight: Female Youth Violence in the Inner City," *Annals of the American Academy of Political and Social Science*, 2004, pp. 32–48.

6. A. Bandura, D. Ross, and S. A. Ross, "Imitation of Film: Mediated Aggressive Models," *Journal of Abnormal Psychology*, 1963, 66, 3–11.

7. C. S. Widom, "The Cycle of Violence," *Science*, 1989, 244, 160–165.

8. R. Reece, *Child Abuse: Medical Diagnosis and Management* (Philadelphia: Lea and Febinger, 1994).

9. Center for Women Policy Studies, *Teen Women Ask Their Peers About Violence, Hate and Discrimination: The Report of the Teen Women Leadership Development Initiative Survey* (Washington, D.C.: Center for Women Policy Studies, 2001).

10. P. Chesler, *Woman's Inhumanity to Woman* (New York: Penguin, 2003).

11. See, for example, L. Eron, L. R. Huesmann, M. M. Lefkowitz, and L. O. Walder, "Does Television Cause Aggression?" *American Psychologist*, 1972, 27, 253–263.

12. Bandura, Ross, and Ross, "Imitation of Film."

13. A. N. Meltzoff, "Imitation of Televised Models by Infants," *Child Development*, 1988, 59, 1221–1229.

14. Turner, Hesse, and Peterson-Lewis, "Naturalistic Studies of the Long Term Effects of Television Violence."

15. W. Wood, F. Y. Wong, and J. G. Chachere, "Effects of Media Violence on Viewers' Aggression in Unconstrained Social Interaction," *Psychological Bulletin*, 1991, 109, 371–383.

16. Ness, "Why Girls Fight."

Chapter Six

1. D. Prothrow-Stith and H. R. Spivak, *Murder Is No Accident: Understanding and Preventing Youth Violence in America* (San Francisco: Jossey-Bass, 2004).
2. Prothrow-Stith and Spivak, *Murder Is No Accident*.

Chapter Seven

1. N. C. Hoover, "National Survey: Initiation Rites and Athletics for NCAA Sports Teams," www.alfred.edu/sports_hazing/howmanyarehazed.html, Aug. 30, 1999.
2. H. Nuwer, *High School Hazing: When Rites Become Wrongs* (New York: Franklin Watts, 2000).
3. D. Olveus, *Bullying at School: What We Know and What We Can Do* (Oxford, UK: Blackwell, 1994), p. 157.
4. M. Talbot, "Mean Girls and the New Movement to Tame Them," *New York Times Magazine*, Feb. 24, 2002, pp. 24–29, 40, 58, 64–65.

Resources

As medical professionals, educators, and parents, we believe it is important for our readers to have access to a great deal of information on the subject of girls and violence. This section offers an inventory of sources from books to Web sites. It is our intent to provide a wide range of information, opinions, and data, whether we agree with the viewpoints offered or not. The provision of this information is not an endorsement on our part of the materials or the interpretations.

We recommend that you use these materials to become informed and knowledgeable, but it is important that you apply your judgment in using them. In particular, the movies and television programs we mention do not necessarily provide the most accurate or desirable images of the issue, and we suggest you view them as starting-off points for discussions with your daughter or other girls and young women about making choices and about how to behave in certain situations in order to avert negative consequences.

Books and Articles

Adler, F. *Sisters in Crime*. New York: McGraw-Hill, 1975.

Artz, S. "Exploring Theories of Female Crime and Delinquency." In *Sex, Power, & the Violent School Girl*. New York: Teachers College Press, 1999.

Bureau of Justice Statistics, National Crime Victimization Survey. "Comparing UCR and NCVS." [http://www.ojp.usdoj.gov/bjs]. 2003.

Campbell, A. "Female Participation in Gangs." In C. R. Huff (ed.), *Gangs in America*. Thousand Oaks, Calif.: Sage, 1990.

Chan, R. K. (1998). "Karate Killed the Monster in Me." In P. Kay, A. Estepa, and A. Desetta (eds.), *Things Get Hectic*. New York: Simon & Schuster.

Chesler, P. *Woman's Inhumanity to Woman*. New York: Penguin, 2003.

Chesney-Lind, M. "Girls' Crime and Woman's Place: Toward a feminist model of female delinquency." *Crime and Delinquency*, 1989, 35(1), 5–29.

Community Violence Prevention Project. *Peace by Piece: A Guide for Preventing Community Violence*. Boston: Harvard School of Public Health, 1998.

Druck, K., Kaplowitz, M., and Blanchard, K. *How to Talk to Your Kids About School Violence*. New York: Onomatopoeia, 2003.

Fried, S., and Fried, P. *Bullies and Victims*. New York: M. Evans, 1996.

Garbarino, J. *Raising Children in a Socially Toxic Environment*. San Francisco: Jossey-Bass, 1995.

Gilligan, C. *In a Different Voice: Psychological Theory and Women's Development*. Cambridge, Mass.: Harvard University Press, 1982.

"Girls and Violence." ERIC Digest No. 143. New York: ERIC Clearinghouse on Urban Education. [www.ericfacility.net/ericdigests/ed430069.html].

Golden, B. *Healthy Anger: How to Help Children and Teens Manage Their Anger*. New York: Oxford University Press, 2003.

"Michigan v. Collier, Patterson . . . Teens Accused of Killing Grandmother." [www.courttv.com/trails/collier/background.html].

Molnar, B. E., and others. "What Girls Need: Recommendations for Preventing Violence Among Urban Girls in the US." *Social Science & Medicine*, forthcoming.

Ness, C. D. "Why Girls Fight: Female Youth Violence in the Inner City." *Annals of the American Academy of Political and Social Science*, 2004, pp. 32–48.

Office of Juvenile Justice and Delinquency Prevention. *Female Delinquency Cases, 1997*. Washington, D.C.: U.S. Department of Justice, 2000.

Oliver, J., and Ryan, M. *Lesson One: The ABCs of Life—The Skills We All Need but Were Never Taught*. New York: Simon & Schuster/Fireside, 2004.

Perlstein, L. *Not Much, Just Chillin': The Hidden Lives of Middle Schoolers*. New York: Farrar, Straus & Giroux, 2003.

Pipher, M. *Reviving Ophelia*. New York: Ballantine, 1984.

Prothrow-Stith, D., and Spivak, H. *Murder Is No Accident: Understanding and Preventing Youth Violence in America*. San Francisco: Jossey-Bass, 2004.

Sampson, R., Raudenbush, S., and Earls, F. "Neighborhoods and Violent Crime: A Multi-Level Study of Collective Efficacy." *Science*, 1997, *277*, 918–924.

Simmons, R. "The Road Ahead." In *Odd Girl Out: The Hidden Culture of Aggression in Girls*. New York: Harcourt, 2002.

Thompson, M., O'Neill, G., and Cohen, L. "Worst Enemies: Social Cruelty in the Lives of Children"; "Still Standing: How Kids Manage Conflict, Betrayal, and Reconciliation." In *Best Friends and Worst Enemies: Understanding the Social Lives of Children*. New York: Ballantine, 2001.

White, E. *Fast Girls*. New York: Berkley, 2002.

Wiseman, R. *Queen Bees and Wannabes*. New York: Three Rivers Press, 2002.

Web Sites

American Academy of Pediatrics
www.aap.org

Boys and Girls Clubs of America
National Office
1230 W. Peachtree Street NW
Atlanta, GA 30309
404-487-5700
www.bgca.org/programs

Break the Cycle
P.O. Box 64996
Los Angeles, CA 90064
310-286-3366 or 888-988-TEEN
www.break-the-cycle.org

Louis D. Brown Peace Institute
1452 Dorchester Avenue, 2nd Floor
Dorchester, MA 02122
617-825-1917

Bureau of Justice Statistics
U.S. Department of Justice, Office of Justice Programs
www.ojp.usdoj.gov/bjs/homicide/intimates.htm

Centers for Disease Control and Prevention
www.cdc.gov/ncipc/pub-res/research_agenda/09_youthviolence.htm

Children's Defense Fund
25 E Street NW
Washington, DC 20001
www.childrensdefense.org

Dads and Daughters
P.O. Box 3458
Duluth, MN 55803
218-722-3942 or 888-824-DADS
www.dadsanddaughters.org

The Empower Program
4420 Connecticut Avenue NW, Suite 250
Washington, DC 20008
202-686-1908
www.empowered.org

Family Tree, Inc.
3805 Marshall Street
Wheat Ridge, CO 80033
303-467-3794, ext. 707
www.thefamilytree.org

The Freda Centre for Research on Violence against Women and Children
www.harbour.sfu.ca/freda/articles/stat2.htm

Girl Scouts
420 Fifth Avenue
New York, NY 10005
800-GSUSA-4-U
www.girlscouts.org

Girls' Circle Association
458 Christensen Lane
Cotati, CA 94931
707-794-9477
www.girlscircle.com

Girls' Coalition of Greater Boston
P.O. Box 930
Boston, MA 02117
617-536-8543
info@girlscoalition.org   www.girlscaolition.org

Girls Incorporated
120 Wall Street
New York, NY 10005
www.girlsinc.org

gURL.com
1440 Broadway, 21st Floor
New York, NY 100018
www.gurl.com

KidsPeace National Centers
KidsPeace Hospital
5300 KidsPeace Drive
Orefield, PA 18069
800-KID-123
www.kidspeace.org

Lesson One Company, Inc.
245 Newbury Street, Suite F

Boston, MA 02116
617-247-2787
www.lessonone.org

The Media Project
www.themediaproject.com

Medical College of Wisconsin
www.healthlink.mcw.edu/article/98409006.html

Movie reviews
www.kidsinmind.com

National Association of School Psychologists
www.nasponline.org/advocacy/youth_violence

National Youth Violence Prevention Resource Center
P.O. Box 10809
Rockville, MD 20849
866-723-3968
www.safeyouth.org

Parents, Media and Public Policy:
A Kaiser Family Foundation Survey
www.kff.org/about/publicopinion.cfm

PEACE ZONE
Harvard School of Public Health,
  Lesson One Company, and Louis D. Brown Peace Institute
www.peacezone.org

Roxbury Youthworks
Female Focus Initiative
www.roxburyyouthworks.org

Southern Poverty Law Center (a sponsor of
  National Youth Violence Prevention Week)
www.splcenter.org/news

TeenCentral
www.teencentral.net

Third Wave Foundation
116 East 16th Street, 7th Floor
New York, NY 10003
212-388-1898
www.thirdwavefoundation.org

UNICEF, Voices of Youth
www.unicef.org

Urban Improv
8 St. John Street
Jamaica Plain, MA 02130
617-232-1175
www.urbanimprov.org
www.aimsmultimedia.com

Dating Violence

American Psychological Association
750 First Street NE
Washington, DC 20002
800-374-2721
www.apa.org/pii/teen/contents

Cool Nurse
www.coolnurse.com/dating

National Center for Victims of Crime
2000 M Street NW
Suite 480
Washington, DC 20036
800-FYI-CALL
www.ncvc.org

National Domestic Violence Hotline
P.O. Box 161810
Austin, TX 78716
800-799-SAFE
www.ndvh.org/teens

Movies and Videotapes

Juvies
Mean Girls
Thirteen
Families for Prevention. "Family Inventory."
Partnerships for Preventing Violence. "Building Bridges: Strengthening Schools
and Communities." Broadcast no. 4, Oct. 15, 1999. Harvard School of Public
Health.
"Respecting Yourself and Others." PeaceTalks series no. 5 (with Michael
Pritchard).

About the Authors

Deborah Prothrow-Stith is a nationally recognized public health leader. As a physician working in inner-city hospitals and neighborhood clinics, she recognized violence as a societal "disease" that could be prevented through implementing effective public health strategies. Appointed commissioner of public health for the Commonwealth of Massachusetts in 1987, she expanded treatment programs for AIDS and drug rehabilitation. During her tenure she also established the first Office of Violence Prevention in a department of public health.

As a chief spokesperson for a national movement to prevent violence, Prothrow-Stith developed a widely acclaimed violence prevention curriculum for schools and communities, Violence Prevention Curriculum for Adolescents, and coauthored *Deadly Consequences* (with M. Weissman, 1991), the first book to present the public health perspective on violence to a mass audience. She is also the author or coauthor of over eighty publications on medical and public health issues, and she served as a member of President Clinton's National Campaign Against Youth Violence. Innovative in her approach to violence prevention, she continues to develop programs and nurture partnerships with community-based programs locally and nationally, including the Community Violence Prevention Project and Partnerships for Preventing Violence, a satellite broadcast training forum.

Prothrow-Stith is associate dean for faculty development and professor of public health practice in the Department of Health Policy and Management at the Harvard School of Public Health. She was the founding director of the Division of Public Health Practice at the Harvard School of Public Health, whose mission is to translate research into practice. She received her B.A. degree from Spelman College and her M.D. degree from Harvard Medical School and has been awarded ten honorary doctorates.

Howard R. Spivak is chief of the Division of General Pediatrics and Adolescent Medicine and vice president for community health programs at the New England Medical Center in Boston, Massachusetts. He is professor of pediatrics and community health at Tufts University School of Medicine and director of the Tufts University Center for Children. He has served as deputy commissioner of public health for the Commonwealth of Massachusetts and, prior to that, as director of adolescent health services for the city of Boston.

Spivak has been involved with activities in youth violence prevention for over twenty years, including cofounding the Boston Violence Prevention Program (the first community-based public health violence prevention program in the nation); the development of the Office of Violence Prevention for the Commonwealth of Massachusetts (the first such initiative at the state level in the nation); the writing of numerous articles, book chapters, and editorials on the issue of violence prevention among youth; participation in numerous studies and evaluations of youth violence prevention efforts; and the development of the first emergency room surveillance initiative for weapon-related injuries. He speaks regularly around the nation on youth violence prevention strategies and engages in ongoing work with many communities in the development of violence prevention programs. He holds a B.A. degree from the University of Rochester and an M.D. degree from the University of Rochester School of Medicine. He is married, with two children, and lives in the Boston area.

Deborah Prothrow-Stith and Howard R. Spivak are also the authors of *Murder Is No Accident: Understanding and Preventing Youth Violence in America* (Jossey-Bass, 2004).

Index

Power plays, 11–12
Power Rangers, 85
Pregnancy, teen, 64
Prevention, 15–16
Professional caregivers, 102–103, 108
Prostitution, 59, 64, 83
Protective factors: and academic
    performance, 74–75; and building
    on success, 72–73; multiple levels
    of operation of, 69–71; and
    nurturing environment, 73–74;
    race and class issues in, 75–76
Prothrow-Stith, D., 16, 17, 58
Prothrow-Stith, M., 16
Prothrow-Stith, P., 16
Punishment, creative. *See* Creative
    punishment
Putdowns, 11–12, 111, 121

Q
"Queen bees," 10, 11, 32, 33
Queen Bees and Wannabes (Wiseman),
    32, 33
Queen Latifah, 84

R
Race, 75–76, 108
*Raising Children in a Socially Toxic
    Environment* (Garbarino), 78
Reaching out, 12–13, 69
Reporting, 43
Respect, 111–112, 125–128
Revenge, 82
Risk factors: biological, 63–64;
    clustered nature of, 59–60; and
    gun availability, 60–61; multiple
    levels of operation of, 69–71; and
    poverty, 61; and social and cultural
    influences, 68–69; and substance
    abuse, 62–63

Role model, 96–100; and bullying,
    111–112; and role playing, 108;
    and schools, 123–125
Rug Rats (television series), 84
Running away, 64, 65, 83

S
Sarandon, S., 84
Scandinavia, 131
School threats, 67–68
Schools: and acting as role model,
    123–135; ART model for,
    123–130; changing experience of,
    120–122; frequently asked ques-
    tions concerning, 130–138; impor-
    tance of, 122; and integrating
    violence prevention into class-
    room, 135–136; as multiservice
    centers, 126–128; and partnerships
    with public service organizations,
    136–138; and reaching out to
    others, 125–128; and reports of
    violence in homes, 138; role of
    parents in, 135; and talking and
    listening, 128–130; tips for,
    119–138
Seattle, Washington, 60
Self-defense, myth of, 31–32
Self-destructive behaviors, 8, 9, 12,
    59, 77–78, 83
Self-esteem, 101
Self-medication, 62
Serotonin, 63–64
Set It Off (cinema), 84
Sex, Power, and the Violent School Girl
    (Artz), 74
Sexism, 108
Sexual abuse, 67–68
Sexual activity, 69
Sexual promiscuity, 59